T0131501

THE JOB SHOPPER

D. BYRON WILEY

BALBOA.
PRESS
A DIVISION OF HAY HOUSE

Balboa Press books may be ordered through booksellers or by contacting:

Balboa Press
A Division of Hay House
1663 Liberty Drive
Bloomington, IN 47403
www.balboapress.com
1 (877) 407-4847

Because of the dynamic nature of the Internet, any web addresses or links contained in this book may have changed since publication and may no longer be valid. The views expressed in this work are solely those of the author and do not necessarily reflect the views of the publisher, and the publisher hereby disclaims any responsibility for them.

The author of this book does not dispense medical advice or prescribe the use of any technique as a form of treatment for physical, emotional, or medical problems without the advice of a physician, either directly or indirectly. The intent of the author is only to offer information of a general nature to help you in your quest for emotional and spiritual well-being. In the event you use any of the information in this book for yourself, which is your constitutional right, the author and the publisher assume no responsibility for your actions.

Any people depicted in stock imagery provided by Thinkstock are models, and such images are being used for illustrative purposes only.
Certain stock imagery © Thinkstock.

Print information available on the last page.

ISBN: 978-1-5043-4716-7 (sc)
ISBN: 978-1-5043-4718-1 (hc)
ISBN: 978-1-5043-4717-4 (e)

Library of Congress Control Number: 2015920689

Balboa Press rev. date: 3/21/2016

TABLE OF CONTENTS

INTRODUCTION

I started this book many years ago, but it took me to this point in my life, to actually write it.

I often hear people say that writing is therapy. Having been a songwriter/composer most of my life, I could actually empathize with *them*. Having written this book, I know what they feel; it is very good therapy.

My original reason for writing this book was to teach people in engineering how to be a contractor, ***effectively***. What I sat down to write and what I have completed are quite a bit different and ***The Job Shopper*** manuscript has evolved and grown.

I possibly could have written several books with this information, so I divided it up into several sections.

- Section 1 - A self-help section told in a "unique manner"
- Section 2- Some wisdom for life.
- Section 3 - A section about professional advancement tactics.
- Section 4 - The business of job shopping
- Section 5 - Examples of people that have to work twice as hard to get half the credit and then need to fight to get the rest

This book can help one navigate very productively through life in whatever your manner of business. It will give you a strong understanding of how the emotions can have an effect on your life, and how someone else's emotions can as well. It will show you how to avoid life's negative distractions and still go through life enjoying oneself. It will show you how to deal with co-workers, supervisors and subordinates effectively. And it will show you how to develop a positive mental attitude and more.

I hope this book enlightens you and helps you become more successful in your life's personal and professional endeavors.

Thank you for reading.

CHAPTER 1

RECOGNIZING AND AVOIDING NEGATIVE PEOPLE.

This chapter has been an area of this manuscript that I really had to motivate myself to write. I do not like to think about these individuals, let alone write about them. However, these people are in our lives every day and most everyone in today's times probably has been one of these types. Thank you for waking up if you made the change or already had it in you.

For several days, my desire and motivation for editing this chapter was low. The thing, as it seems to me, is that the more you pay attention to these people the more you become like them. To avoid people that can cause you moral harm you must be aware of whom they are. No one can read minds but you can get pretty close. Some behavior patterns are hard wired to some emotions. So you can pretty much assure yourself that if someone displays a series of negative emotions, you need to eliminate that person from your life immediately. The longer they stay a part of your life the more damage they will do to your moral fiber or worse. I listed some to get you started. I am sure I missed some, but hey, you have to start somewhere.

Ever been in a conversation and someone just starts to talk over you and interrupt you every chance they get? They seem to get upset the more you try to finish your conversation. People like this don't care what you are thinking, they don't want others to know or hear what you want to say, they may be attempting to outshine you, or some combination of or possibly all of the above.

They don't care what you have to offer, unless they want to steal something from you and take the credit later. The bottom line is they have absolutely no respect for you. Now that you are aware that these people exist and what they are capable of, you must start noticing ***behavior, body language and actions***.

For example; the face never lies, so try this. Start smiling at everyone and notice what happens. Show the person with your smile that you only feel positive things about them. That person is compelled to smile back, if they have no negative feelings for you. If they do feel negative feelings for you, the smile will be forced or they will force themselves to not smile. Also watch them and pay close attention to their eyes. If the eye muscles move upward then it is a positive smile, if the eyes don't this person is possibly deceiving you and possesses a negative disposition about you. This is the quickest way to gauge if a person feels positive or negative emotions for you. Also, once you become good at reading facial expressions you can almost read a person's mind. Continue this ritual to see if there are changes in the person and to constantly monitor how you stand with them. Also keep in mind smiling a lot, keeps you healthy, helps you stay positive and causes people to have positive emotions for you. Also, if you are a rich minority athlete, or celebrity, you seem to earn a lot more income.

Try to always recognize people that tend to speak negatively about other people. The ones that are constantly criticizing for no productive reason. In hip hop we called them the ***Haters***. Keep in mind cracking or jabbing does not make a person a hater unless done with a negative mindset. Some people will target a person because of jealousy and envy and try to make them look bad or possibly embarrass them. It's like the old saying, "They want to dim or even put your light out so theirs can shine brighter".

People that are condescending are usually very insecure and need to be negative or even sadistic to feel relevant. Others tend to lie for negative reasons and are just evil. Inconsiderate, disrespectful and selfish individuals don't consider how one feels and attempt to find a 'mark' or victim and use them. Some people will tell you that, "you can't", or "you won't". I had an aquaintance like this. I don't talk to her anymore. As a matter of fact, I don't deal with most of my relative's or past friends anymore and I owe that to the character of <u>Willie Lynch</u> who in my opinion, if he really existed, would be the King of Haters. It was said that in a speech he gave, that if the slave owners listened to him and did like he instructed, the descendants of <u>NON</u> would perpetually hate each other for 400 years. The Slave owners listened....and it worked.

Some people love to see other people that try to succeed, fail and will always volunteer bad advice to hurt someone's efforts. People that use a fake warm smile regularly can never be trusted under any circumstances. I tend to try to not trust anyone, but some people you have to trust at times. Make sure you pick them properly. Don't use your heart, use the concepts in this book. Some people appear to be all that you want in a friend, companion or business acquaintance. They seem to have your back like they can sense your struggle. They seem to know just when to come to your rescue. With anyone, one must pay close attention to what they say and do to determine what is false about them and what is real. I appreciate being a fly on the wall and listening to people speak about me when they don't know I am there. There is no better way of determining if a person is two-faced or what type of agenda they have. Some of these people may display multiple emotions toward you, in a short span of time, when there has been little or no change in your personality. These people are unstable and should be avoided, until they show some emotional stability.

At times in life we do things that we enjoy. When one enjoys something they tend to do it whenever they can. Sometimes these desires for something become uncontrollable. At that point a person falls into one of the negative person categories. Manmade drugs, alcohol, a poor diet, negative sex, gambling etc. are negative devices that can have horrible effects, and may possibly destroy anyone close to them, regardless of if the person that gets hurt, indulges in these negativities or not.

Another type of person one should avoid is a person that walks away from you in the middle of your conversation with them and is not angry. They obviously don't care what you have to say. They find no intellectual value from your conversation. They consider you inferior. This is something I experience to this day. Very recently a supervisor had done this to me and he actually asked a question and then walked off before I could answer him fully. Some people aren't evil but we must put them in this category because they can hinder someone's growth, depending on the subordinate's weaknesses.

Some haters are not bad haters if that is actually possible. Some of them can just be closed minded. They won't believe the truth if it smacked them in the face. This is extremely important, because this one weakness in one person can destroy a whole team. A person or a group of people has to have the ability to evolve and improve. If as many as one of them is stuck on stupid, they will sink the whole ship or cause it to never make progress. This will give any wise person a good excuse to leave or quit. Keep this in mind; if someone can have negative emotions for someone else, they are capable of having those same emotions for you. One of the most dangerous negative people, has no idea that they are even causing you harm. Here is a list of some negative individuals.

- The Drama Lover
- The Never Happy
- D. Bully
- False Faces (Two Face and Many Faces

The Drama Lover...

Off the top of my head there are four types of Drama Lovers...

- The first of the four is the ***Insta Gator***. This individual enjoys getting other people to do negative things. They are like a negative cheer leader or coach, because some will even demonstrate what they want to happen. Watch out for these individuals. They may hide behind someone else. Even get someone else to speak or front for them. The one thing you can count on is they will definitely leave someone else holding the bag.
- The ***Perpitraitor*** is the culprit that actually does the negative actions. He or she is the most dangerous of all. Sometimes these

individuals are gullible. Sometimes they have been harboring a need to do something negative and an ***Insta Gator*** befriends them and it's on!

- The ***Spec Tator*** aka Agitator, will cheer and incite. They seem to get more courage as their numbers grow. Some can evolve into the previous two characters in the ideal circumstance. These individuals watching or witnessing an event give the previous two characters an audience in which to perform for.

- And I can't forget the ***Self Hater***. This is an individual that wallows in self-pity. Their life is completely based off what other's tell them. They lack self-confidence and self-worth. They are easily swayed to a new opinion. Often suicidal and have no problem sacrificing themselves for an ***Insta Gator's*** cause.

It seemed obvious to call the next group of negative individuals ***The Never Happy***.

Why, because, they are never happy. Here are three people that seem to never be satisfied no matter how much you try to help them or how much is done for them.....

- The first is the ***Spoiled brat***. This is a childlike person. They need and want you to do, what they want to do, when they want you to. Or just like a child, you are likely to witness them throw a fit or tantrum.

- Next is the ***User***. The User can be a truly sinister person that understands and has empathy for others, but uses it to see weakness in their prey. They usually have no compassion or respect for their target.

- One negative type, I am sure you have known is the ***Complainer***. The Complainer can only see negative. They seem to be blind to the bright side. Even if there is something that is obviously good to say, they find it very hard to not say something negative.

D. Bully – There are many types of bullies. Most recently, ***Cyber Bullies*** have emerged as a heavily spoken about topic of conversation. I thought I would delve a little deeper and examine some personality types. Here are four that came to mind for me.

- **The Reluctant Bully.** This type of bully is someone that would not be a bully normally. They need a reason to walk this course of negative dominance. The **Insta Gator** loves this type of Bully to get a plan into motion.
- **The Power Driven Bully.** This is someone that doesn't care about any person that happens to get in their way. They will get rid of that person any way they see fit.
- **The Insecure Bully** has fears, phobias and secrets to protect. If anyone gets near the object or secret, it will unleash **The Insecure Bully's** anger and rage.
- The last type of bully I came up with is, the **Controlling Bully.** They always feel the need to be in charge. It doesn't matter if they are the best for the job or not. They could be the worst for it, but still feel the need to control anything, or anyone, within their grasp.

Sometimes people feel the need to deceive and put on **False Faces** in order to accomplish things they need in life. Because of their need I had a need to write these next two sections.

The first is **Two Face**—

Two Face is usually a double agent but only for their own causes. They often pretend to be someone's friend only to use their trust to get information they can use any way they deem fit. They will also say one thing to you and say another thing away from you.

The second I called **Many Faces**—

Many Faces could be a positive or negative individual. They seem to have multiple personalities. Sometimes they may even seem crazy. Some are very stable and use planned mood swings to accomplish a goal, while others may actually be a degree of schizophrenia. These are the people that you meet with sometimes and you have no idea what mood they might be in when they arrive.

This next category is truly a devastating thing for any human to be a victim of. The one thing that is given to us that can never be taken away is our ability to think and make rational choices in life. However, some very evil men created ways that people can involuntarily give up this power over ourselves and surrender it to a devastating and life threatening type of habit. I called this victim, *D. Addict*.

D Addict truly worships a higher power. I will dig deeper into this subject matter later in the chapter on Man Made Drugs. D. Addict lives by the motto, misery loves company and has no problem offering their habit to you. Here are five examples of *D. Addict*—

- *The Manmade Zombie* is anyone that has developed an addiction for a manmade drug or chemical. From your standard Methamphetamine users, the different cocaine users, the heroin addicts to the alleged bath salt junkie that the South Florida Police shot and killed for eating another man alive. These people have become victim to a population control trap.....Imagine a small bug in a sink of water that is being drained
- *Al Key Hawlic* is anyone that allows their drinking habit to cause extreme negative problems in their life in one or more of these five areas; health, family, professional, financial and legal
- *Dee Blunt* is a person that feels they can't smoke marijuana without it being rolled in a cigar. The reason for this is cigars are very addictive in a similar manner as cigarettes. They also cause one to smoke 4-5 times more marijuana than a person normally would. The biggest problem with this is cigars cause heart failure.
- *New Porter*-A *New Porter* is a menthol cigarette smoker. Menthol is an ingredient that stimulates receptors in the throat and gives one a fresh breath taste similar to peppermint. People that smoke menthol cigarettes, tend to inhale larger amounts of smoke with each puff due to this taste. Cigarette smoke contains over 4,000 chemicals, including 43 that are known to cause cancer and 400

other toxins. They contain nicotine, tar, and carbon monoxide, formaldehyde, ammonia, hydrogen cyanide, arsenic, and DDT.

Nicotine is very addictive. So the **New Porter** is at a higher risk of cancer than a non-menthol smoker. An ex=girlfriend of mine was a cigarette smoker since she was a teenager. She passed away due to complications from lung cancer, caused by menthol cigarette smoking in her mid-forty's.

- *Kay Seeno* is the person that is addicted to gambling. Another topic I will discuss in detail in a later chapter

- *Nie Eve N. Clueless......*The *Nie Eve N. Clueless* are people that are ignorant and unaware of the negative they do. Some of these types have a pure and very strong element of compassion. It is so strong that it blinds them of the ability to empathize with the individual they are dealing with and they may often disrespect them. It is the old cliché' too much of a good thing can be bad'. Some of these individuals can be helped, while others are so far gone you need to just let them be, period

- *Crab Enda Barrel*-Jealousy and envy are emotions that can consume a person's desire and motivation. In the Bible it is called Coveting. *Crab Enda Barrel* is an individual that can't stand to see someone else do well. I came up with three types—

  - *Talk Yadown*-Talk Yadown is the negative motivator. Always coming up with reasons to hold you back or derail your efforts through conversation

  - *Pull Yadown*-This person will stand in your way, sabotage you or actually pull you down

  - *Beat Yadown*-Well this is obvious, this person will go as far as kill you to stop you from doing better than them

  - *Rob Ya Blind*- is a high ranking official of the anti-Two Way Street principal movement....Here are three.....

    - That Mutha Fucka......is a lover or spouse that takes a lot more than they give and sometimes deserts their lover and leaves them with nothing of value

- Yo Potna......is a business associate or a friend that is willing to destroy a friendship or business venture for non-logical or selfish reasons
- Yo Gubna, also known as the Shepherd or The People Programmers. They are the Organizations and Groups in command and have dominion over human society....

I gave them funny names, so it would become a labor of love for you, to recognize these people, and in some cases get a few laughs out of doing what's best for you. Please do this with an open minded, non-judgmental approach. Otherwise I will have to create another negative description, for your newly created category. Some of these negative types can be helped, although if you decide you want to help them you must proceed with wisdom and caution. Some are hopeless and you should avoid them as if they have the plague. In some cases they do, literally to the death. There are other negative people, but these are very common ones and as I said previously, this is a good place to start.

CHAPTER 2

RECOGNIZING AND ATTRACTING POSITIVE PEOPLE.

This pool of individuals I am about to describe are the candidates for the type of person you want to recruit into your inner circle. I will speak in depth about the inner circle in a forthcoming chapter.

These people won't advertise who they are. The people I am about to describe are the people one must recognize and attract. You need to protect these types from the ones in the previous chapter, and always do what you can, to keep their weaknesses from showing around negative individuals. They are prey, a potential victim for the wrong or negative thinker.

When creating your inner circle make sure these are the types of people that you populate its positions with. They don't have to ever come in contact with each other or ever meet. They are your cabinet and you are the president of your own destiny. So make sure any consigliore you choose has some of these qualities. The ones with access to your ear and personal space need to be positive or you will eventually turn negative yourself without even realizing it. The ones that are generous and unselfish must be protected from the snakes and the wolves that prey on them.

Some people just love giving money to people that need help. Unfortunately there are negative people that make a living off extorting money from these people. They are looked upon as suckers, victims or an easy mark. That is why I say when you bring these types into your inner circle, always protect them and not let them be exposed to possible harm. Never take advantage of them...They are an insurance policy, but one must always try to give back, even when the person doesn't want you too.

You must study them, determine what they always appreciate and do that in return for the help they give. No one will stay around someone that doesn't give back unless they are foolish or the victim type. The victim type needs to be protected and sheltered, because they have sort of a Stockholm syndrome about helping people.

Some positive people are very warm and a strong commodity when a part of your inner circle. Their smile, their touch, the warmth you feel when you get close to them, are the signs that will allow you to recognize them. You will feel the need to hug them. Listen to them speak. They can look at you and you want to be with them. Their warmth can be a human magnet. They are great for recruiting and encouraging the people that you want in your inner circle.

These people's eyes seem to stare through you as if they see you naked. Well actually they kind of do. They know when someone is attracted to them and have the ability to change a person's mood in a positive manner which is a great asset to anyone's inner circle. Compassion and empathy are such wonderful emotions when someone feels them both.

Some people have a wealth of these emotions and feel the need to do for others relentlessly. They are the ones that don't mind doing favors and not looking for anything in return. They volunteer at soup kitchens and do things for the homeless. They also take on noble causes that have no reward for them. Their reward for them is seeing someone smile with relief because a major problem has been solved. They will seek out people to help at times. These people love a good charity, and enjoy raising monies for good causes. They seem to not mind sacrificing themselves or their worldly possessions to fight for a cause. They refuse to be selfish and choose to be selfless.

With age, one usually develops wisdom. Some people are naturally gifted with it. Some develop it through life's experiences. Anyone that accumulates knowledge and then wants to share what they learned is a blessing to anyone's inner circle.

Throughout history creative people have used self-expression, packaged in an art form, to cause people to change moods. Here are a few positive examples of these types of people at work.

Maya Angelo would write flowing poetic masterpieces that can and will enlighten and inspire one. Her poem *I Know why the Caged Bird Sings* is a very emotional and symbolic comparison of two birds. One that is completely free in mind, body and spirit and can go and do as it pleases, while in contrast the other bird is caged and can only dream of what the other bird can literally take for granted. One bird can achieve all that he can believe, and one feels a feeling of defeat every time they open their eyes in the morning. One plans what the day will bring, while the other wishes for a different circumstance. One sings for pleasure and the other sings for freedom and mental survival.

Having been a songwriter for years I appreciate artistry and the freedom of expression. I often think back to the days of the story teller songwriters and still enjoy listening to these same songs today when I need an emotional lift in my mood.

Every now and then a musical artist pens a good record edifying someone positive or had a major impact on society. One such artist was Arrested Development. They used Hip Hop to lift a people's spirit. In their record **Mr. Wendal**, **Mr. Wendal** represents the homeless man that everyone has seen that just kind of minds his own business, maybe pushing a grocery store cart or sitting down having a drink. Society has basically cast him out of the main populous and left him to fend for himself. He goes through life disrespected for the most part, but can always give you insight into most things that we working stiffs take for granted.

Mr. Wendal loves the opportunity to trade his knowledge and wisdom for some change. One can never look a gift horse in the mouth. The person that doesn't ask for much or anything in return to share their wisdom with you is someone that should be sought out at times to stimulate mental growth and awareness.

Maintaining a positive mental attitude is mandatory, to achieve anything you desire in life. ***Bobby McFerrin's Don't Worry, Be Happy*** was a number one jam. Shunned by most of the Black People I knew, because we had negative mind sets, McFerrin's classic was looked upon as a joke or gimmick record. Listening to it today, I realize that this type of thinking is the back bone of this book. One must never let worry or fear creep into our hearts and minds, we must fill ourselves with the positive emotions. And every now and then play Mr. McFerrin's classic or just hum it to yourself. Recently I needed a boost in moral and positive energy and I played the video. In one of the early scenes, Mr. Mc Ferrin pretends to jump from a window........and I paused..... I wish Robin Williams would of sung this song maybe one more time.

Some people care more for the greater good than their own selfish wants or needs. These people understand what the term, team player means. One type of team player is someone that doesn't mind someone else getting the credit, but will work harder than anyone else at times. They realize it's a team effort and show humility and always point to the accomplishments of their team mates when the team has success no matter how much they contribute. They appreciate the art of the assist. Imagine an NBA point guard that doesn't care about shooting. The player wants to win and enjoys being a part of something great or successful and doesn't need to shine.

Other individuals to seek out are people that have the natural ability to make you laugh. An inner circle at times needs to unwind. They need to kick back and no one can cause this to happen more than someone that is humorous. A good joke can spread infectious positivity to anyone close enough to hear it. When building your inner circle, seek out people that recognizes someone's worth, or greatness, doesn't kiss ass, but has no problem acknowledging and edifying someone that deserves it. They are neither a yes man, nor a no man. They will speak in a manner that honestly improves the scenario or circumstance. They will deal with people in a manner that is never conceived as condescending or arrogant. They have a very confident humility and can mix these emotions extremely well. They are careful to never let one dominate the other and maintain the balance between the two emotions at all times.

Every inner circle needs a voice of reason. One that shows fairness and is the perfect judge or person to help with a dispute or settlement. They will attempt to stay neutral in a manner to cause every one present to be happy with an outcome. They can negotiate between the parties because they empathize with everyone involved. They will not let their emotions or loyalties affect their conscious choices or statements.

Some individuals are very organized. Everyone needs an organized friend. They will help you stay on schedule. They will help you come prepared. They will put your ducks in a row at times when you are running blind, so you don't fall on your face. Keep in mind that if someone has compassion for you, they will allow you to use them positively, to help you in life. They can also help you plan tasks and objectives more effectively.

Another type of person to look for is one with integrity and moral fiber. They will be your conscience at times and help you go to bed every night knowing you did no one harm or anything negative to anyone. They are the people whose eyes one must see when they have a moral dilemma. They are good for helping you make that critical decision that is difficult at times, for some to do on their own.

People that want to nurture, like to Mother you. They are extremely compassionate. They will identify your weaknesses and develop the desire to turn them into strengths. Do not develop pride when dealing with this ally. They are only there to help. When they feel they can't help you, they will probably move along to try to find someone else they can help that will appreciate them. Let them nurture you. If you want to keep them around, create weaknesses that they can engulf themselves into and that will keep them focused on you.

The emotion of sex should be considered when developing your inner circle. At least one in your circle should be an intimate/sexual partner. Choose this person with extreme caution. They will have access to your sub-conscious mind, so they must have a compatible, objective and warm demeanor towards you. You need to develop compassion, empathy and respect for this person. They must possess this for you or show a willingness to develop them all... This person will hear your pillow talk and will hear you talk in your sleep. They will learn things about you that you don't know about yourself. They will know all of your weaknesses and know all of your strengths. They can build you up, or knock you down and destroy you. Always think before you leap. This person cannot be chosen with the third leg, or your moist pink friend. This is how we all have chosen this person at some time in the past most likely.

This person must not be chosen because they have a pleasing smile or a face that's easy on the eyes. They must be chosen by how this person feels about you. How the person acts towards you. They never annoy you. They seem to know what you will say before you say it. They laugh at your humor only when it is funny. Let you know when you are not. You feel their warmth whenever you are near them. They can be homely but you still want to kiss or hold them. There is a chemistry you are looking for but it is an internal feeling that this person will give you. It will be similar to a falling in love feeling when you recognize them and they have made themselves known to you. Cherish this person. They may end up being your spouse or significant other.

Positive people pay attention to the big picture. They are not concerned with winning every battle but prefer to plan and strategize on the winning of the war. They don't sweat the small things and have the ability to let go of negative things in the past. Everyone makes mistakes in life. They can make fun of themselves and laugh about mistakes and failures.

A big reason positive people maintain a positive attitude is through laughter. There is humor everywhere and a positive person will see it and make light of it causing everyone in hearing distance to laugh or smile. Being goofy or joking around will help people focus on the good things. Positive people take time for themselves; to play, work out, have sex, meditate, pray, rest, sleep, do yoga or deep breathing exercises to eliminate stress and anxiety and to keep a calm and peaceful disposition.

CHAPTER 3

THE POSITIVE EMOTIONS

Positivity is very contagious. It is one of the few addictions in this life that is actually good for you in most cases. The positive emotions should be looked for and embraced always.

People that habitually use the positive emotions should be the only type of people that you allow close to you. With anything, one must use wisdom to avoid excess. Too much of a good thing turns good into bad. I will speak about these scenarios later.

Recently I decided that I wanted to only embrace positive emotions. From my studies and my own personal experience, I realize that feeling positive is physically, spiritually and mentally good for you. Some scientists believe it will extend life. This tends to make sense. If you love life and are happy, you will fight for your life as well as for the people and things in it. When I smile I actually feel better. When I feel the happiest I have fewer concerns. So I strive to stay positive as much as I can. Good moods do wonderful things for meditation.

Using the positive emotions is a daily task. I work on myself every day to try and purge negative emotions as soon as they enter my mind or have a negative effect on my moods. Every human being is "human", which means we are flawed. We will be victims to a negative emotion attack. I developed a few tricks to help me out in these moments. Certain songs, thoughts, poems, memories, humor or anything I can think of that will bring a smile to mine or someone else's face, is my plan of attack and to delete negative emotions, once they develop, or try to change my mood.

Using the positive emotions has many benefits. Too many to even count or categorize. People have the ability to choose and that makes the benefits infinite. In this chapter I will look in detail at some of the positive emotions. There are many more than I can name in this short work and some yet felt or thought of, but the study of the basics is a wonderful way to becoming a better person.

Love – It is the act of having feelings of affection for someone. These feelings can also exhibit the desire for sex with that person. What use to confuse me was if love is a positive emotion then why do some people run when someone tells them they love them? I lost quite a few good women because I told them I loved them. This was very confusing to me. I meant them no harm; no ill will. The reason they run is because there is a difference between loving someone and falling in love with someone and there are two types of falling in love. One is good and one is bad.

To love someone is a good thing for both people. To fall in love with someone should be a good thing for both people, but here is why it isn't. In this country, we mix and confuse all three loves into one type. I have known women that have emigrated from other countries to this one and I have heard them say we use the word love recklessly.

In this country we are taught as children that love should bring with it several negative emotions laying in the cut like a postal worker waiting for a reason to go postal. They are insecurity, the fear of losing the person's love and attention, jealousy, anger, revenge and hate. These emotions will mess up a soup sandwich. One must learn to love with positive emotions rather than these awful negative ones. One must delete all negative emotions from their very being.

When I was naive I realize I reeked of the negative emotions because women would say, all of a sudden, I would start acting weird. That meant I was displaying one or a combination of these negative emotions. Most likely knowing me, it was the fear of losing the woman's love and or attention. I was most certainly guilty of jealousy, revenge and I know everyone from this country that reads this book can say at some time or another they cursed and said they hate someone they were actually in love with.

Love is the most wonderful emotion of all and I didn't have to get in touch with my feminine side to realize that. It is also the second most powerful emotion; second only to sex. With any power one must think, act and proceed wisely prior to its use.

Compassion - Compassion is a feeling of wanting to care for and about someone. Compassion is an emotion perfect for a romantic, intimate or sexual relationship. Although compassion is a sibling of Love, it is not like love per say and it doesn't travel with any negative emotions. An extreme positive example of compassion is what a Mother feels for her child, when the child needs her help.

A marriage will fail if there is no compassion. The term for better or worse is in the vows to get one to commit to being compassionate in a marriage. If someone is sick, hungry, in trouble, etc. One who has compassion for them would be willing to assist them in a positive manner to help solve their problems.

Two people with compassion for each other can have a very wonderful relationship. One should use compassion as a measuring device to determine if they should start an intimate or romantic relationship with someone. It sure wouldn't hurt in a sexual relationship as well. Dirty minds can unite in positive harmony.

Empathy - the feeling that you understand and share another person's experiences, feelings and emotions. It is the ability to look at a person's face or hear their voice and literally share their feelings. The feeling of knowing and realizing that someone is empathetic to you as a person or one of your desires or goals is priceless. You can build a bridge between the two minds to form a better mind. Empathy is an emotion perfect for a romantic, intimate or sexual relationship.

As in electricity when you add more batteries to an existing battery or group of batteries, you produce more power. Same as the human mind. Two people empathetic to each other's needs can sense what the other person wants or needs often before the person feeling the things does. The wonderful thing about Empathy is, it brings compassion with it, along with hope and peace checking things out from a distance, chillin' for a chance to get involved. Ain't nothing wrong with positive emotions coming in clusters.

Respect – It is the feeling of admiring someone or something that is good, valuable, important, etc.: It is the understanding or belief that someone or something is important, serious, worthwhile, and should be treated in an appropriate way.

Respect must be earned. An example of this is when a woman feels it is her right to expect and experience chivalry from a man. Chivalry is a form of respect that a man shows a woman he wishes to bring into his life in an intimate, possibly romantic way. So under these circumstances he should not show chivalry to just any woman he meets or comes across. He should only show it to the women that come into his life that he has desires to share his life with. Not everyone deserves to be respected and not every woman should be shown chivalry. One's actions or position in life must demand respect in order for respect to be deserved. Any sound relationship must contain respect or it is destined to fail. No fruit can grow from a relationship that lacks respect.

In my opinion, the combination of compassion, empathy and respect are mandatory in any relationship, whether sexual, intimate or platonic. All relationships must use these three emotions as a foundation to build on. Any other combination of emotions will cause failure.

A couple must care for each other. If one doesn't the other will develop feelings of neglect or even feel they are being used or taken advantage of. If the relationship lacks empathy the couple will randomly hurt each other whether intentionally or not. And last, but not least, if there is no respect, sooner or later someone will get angry, and anger in most cases will create hate.

The wonderful thing about this combination of emotions is when they are used together in a positive way; they don't need any other emotion to produce a healthy and satisfying relationship. Applying any other positive emotion will only make the relationship better....

Hope - the desire of wanting something to happen or to be true. Hope is a wonderful emotion because it gives one an emotional life. It stimulates ones desires and initiates faith. Hope is an extremely powerful emotion when put into use.

Two examples of hope used as a powerful weapon come to mind. Martin Luther King and Mahatma Gandhi used hope, combined with Faith and Belief as a catalyst. A catalyst to stir up the desire in many people to want to be treated as equals and break free of other people wanting to control them for financial gain due to greed, hate, insecurities and other negative emotions in their enemy's personalities.

Their enemies ruled and controlled people thru propaganda, misinformation, lies and extreme violence. By utilizing hope in a non-violent and non-negative manner they were able to defeat evil and very negative foes without war or taking up arms against their enemies. Thus peace was the result of proper utilization of hope... Unfortunately, Dr. King's hope may have died with him, because soon after his assassination the principals of Willie Lynch were resurrected in the hearts of the descendants of <u>NON</u>.

Peace - a state of tranquility, quiet and serenity. Peace will allow for harmony in all relationships. This is the emotion you should give your mind, body and soul the rest to regroup. Peace must be courted and maintained for those times when one just needs to catch their breath or clear their minds.

One must attempt to have peace in consciousness as well as peaceful sleep. Peace is always used as the positive weapon to combat war. During the sixties people used peace to protest wrongs in our society. "Give Peace a chance", was the cry. They used peace to argue the insanity of Vietnam as well as other wars and military conflicts.

War should not be a solution, but once one person picks up a stick then you need to defend yourself. This all reminds me of children on the playground. If I can't get my way I will beat you up. War is the systematic act of planned mass murder and the people that use war for financial gain are mass murderers for profit. It is what it is. Kind of like the cigarette manufacturers and some food producers. Mass murderers. Timothy McVeigh and other mass murderers killed many people, but who has and will do the most killing? How wonderful this world would be if we could just put down our big stick and seriously give Peace a chance.

Positive Sex - Sex as a positive emotion is a force that causes one to desire intimacy with a person in order to reproduce and start a family. It is also part of the process of the merging of mind, body and soul between two people that care about each other. When two people that love each other become sexual they create a common or emotional bond between them and become, smarter, wiser and empathetic of each other.

Positive sex will cause one to rush home to feel the warmth of their lover. Positive sex will make a man be late for work because he just couldn't quite pull away from his lady without making love to her one more time that morning. To complicate matters more, sometimes he gets so sexually worked up during the work day, he must call his wife and tell her how he is feeling about her. You know what I mean. He may tell her something like, "I'm going to beat dat ass up when I get home". Or maybe he is more of the romantic type and tells her how wonderful making love to her was that morning and he can't stop thinking about her. Positive sex is very essential to maintaining a solid and balanced mentality. It creates confidence, eliminates stress and increases emotional bonds between two people. Most of all I don't think there is anything in life that can be more enjoyable. Positive Sex is a gift from whatever or whomever you call God or the Creator of man and earth. That gift is, the act of reproducing. Positive Sex is the only way two people should have children. This scenario will provide a solid parental structure for the off spring while taking care of them in a loving, caring and nurturing environment. Since there are three types of sex. One positive, one negative and one is an action emotion, then there are three ways to reproduce. Once you read the sections of chapter 4 and 5 on the other two types of sex, come back to this section. Think about the environment these emotions create and how that will effect a child and you will understand fully, why I say women should only be impregnated via positive sex.

CHAPTER 4

THE NEGATIVE EMOTIONS

Misery loves company, and people that engage in these next set of emotions, are your kryptonite. They will steal, kill and destroy you and everything you own, create or care about. Their words are a lethal poison and should never get near your ears if at all possible. They are the foundation of a negative person's moral core as are the positive emotions to someone that is positive. The mind can only be positive or negative. It can't be both, because if one positive or negative emotion enters your mind, more of the same are close behind.

The negative emotions should be avoided at all cost, however in the defense of one's mental stability, loved ones, reputation, material items and accomplishments, one may need to call on them temporarily to defeat a circumstance, hurdle or enemy. However one must delete this emotion as soon as it is no longer needed, and resist any of the negative emotional companions from entering one's mind that rode with the negative emotion, that was used. My advice is if you can avoid using them, then do so. This concept is always a last resort and should never under any circumstances be relied upon or used as a crutch for confidence or any move of advancement.

The negative emotions usually cost more to use than they are worth and can give one pyrrhic victories. Three example's in history when all of the negative emotions were used on a major scale at once, are when 50-100 million people were murdered during the years of manifest destiny and the survivor's lost any hope of retaining their conventional way of life back again. Greed, envy, jealousy, anger and hate were all used in Manifest Destiny. The people that actually did the crimes were diluted into believing the people they were killing and forcing to live another way of life, were sub-human or maybe even animals in some cases.

Imagine you are walking down your street. You notice a hundred dollar bill in a man's hand. Since you are a good person the thought of stealing it never crosses your mind. By contrast if you see a very friendly dog run up to you with a hundred dollar bill in their mouth, what would you do? Yes you would take the money. This is the misinformation that these people were brain washed with to get them to participate in good conscience with Manifest Destiny. During World War Two, some 11 - 17 million Jewish people were killed in all manners of horrible ways by NAZI Germany. I believe the mind of Adolf Hitler was infested with negative emotions, such as; fear, anger, hate, greed, envy and jealousy. The United States displayed many negative emotions when it bombed innocent people in Japan during WWII, that had absolutely nothing to do with Japan's government policies. Once ignited the radiation from Little Boy as the weapon was called, burned the skin off women and children and roasted them alive. People in the United States celebrated the so-called victory. There was very little public empathy for these innocent victims.

Hate - is the act of having a very strong feeling of dislike for someone or something. The emotion of hate can give one an awful feeling which will overwhelm a person as long as they allow this emotion to exist within them. I have noticed that I haven't ever really seen a hateful person smile much. Like all emotions it is extremely contagious and can cause major upheavals in society, families and between friends or acquaintances. Hate can stimulate animosity between co-workers, siblings and friends. It can cause people to take sides in a negative stance or alliance against each other. Hate can never be allowed to materialize or grow. It must be stamped out in the mind with positive thoughts before it festers. Hate is usually a byproduct of anger, envy and jealousy. Hate is infused into the collective mindset of a country when that country is at war with another to stimulate an artificial hate for the enemy and an artificial Empathy for the hero soldiers, by the populous. I have often wondered since Jesus Christ had wool hair, burnt bronze skin and was a Jew, how can some people hate Jews or brown skinned or nappy headed people? Maybe it's Hate's cousin Jealousy. There is no place for either emotion in society.

Anger - Anger is a strong feeling of being upset or annoyed. Possibly because of something wrong or bad, someone has done to you or someone or something that you care about. It will install the feeling that makes someone want to hurt other people or cause one to consider revenge as a solution to satisfying anger's hunger. I can only condone this emotion in a defensive tactic when you need it for strength and confidence to destroy an enemy. When a person is angry they tend to lose control of themselves by losing their patience, wisdom, intelligence and ability to accurately rationalize a situation. Ever noticed if you get mad at someone in the morning it kind of ruins your day emotionally?

Revenge - Revenge is the act of doing something to cause negative events in someone's life because you believe that person did something that hurt you, someone or something you care about or caused you or them hardship. First off remember the saying two wrongs don't make a right, whenever this despicable emotion attempts to ooze its way into your thoughts. Just suppose the other party has allowed revenge to consume them. When would this cycle of potential negative stop? How much pain needs to be inflicted to cause this to end and peace is restored. It could develop into a perpetual cycle of violence. Ask any gang member or the country of Israel and the Palestinians.

Envy - Envy is the feeling of wanting to have what someone else has. This is a waste of a human beings time. If one can take the time to develop thoughts of desire, why not use this negative emotion to stimulate positive opposites to acquire the object of one's desire or someone or something similar. Envy is only good as a desire fire starter, other than that its usage can only lead to a negative outcome.

Jealousy - Jealousy is an action or reactionary emotion. There are three types of jealousy. One type of Jealousy is Envy's evil twin. Another type is the negative feeling humans can get when they find out someone wants or desires the same person, plan or the same object that they desire. The last is the most volatile and can lead to any number of amazingly tragic or dangerous scenarios. The negative feeling a person gets when they feel or know their spouse or significant other is sleeping with or has feelings for someone else.

Sometimes humans feel this emotion for a person even when there is no relationship between them. It is as all negative emotions, an unhappy or angry feeling. It is a feeling that can be caused by the belief that someone you love (such as your husband or wife) has a romantic or sexual interest in someone else or has slept or is sleeping around. This type of jealousy in my opinion is the number one cause of divorce. The number one cause of children living in two different households and essentially living a double life as a child.

I am not hating on the concept of a child having the possibility or potential to have four or more parents, which could be very positive for a child's upbringing, but it could also expose a child to a person on a regular basis that one of the parents would not approve of.

This concept can be either extremely positive or extremely negative, for all involved. In most cases without me actually doing the research I would hypothesize, with the paranoia of some people I imagine it could be pretty negative at times.

Jealousy can give one a feeling of helplessness. It is also the emotion Cain had for his brother Abel in the Old Testament. It was so strong in Cain that he developed hate and anger for his brother and murdered him because of these negative emotions.

Fear - In the words of FDR, We have nothing to fear except fear itself. One must never fear anything life brings to the table. Not death, loss of someone that is cared about, poverty, ill health, old age or any other circumstance that would be considered negative or even tragic. Fear begets worry and nothing in this life is worth the huge cost of worry. It is an unpleasant emotion caused by being aware of a possible or impending danger: a feeling of being afraid has only one good quality and that is causing you to think with your sixth sense, because the need to survive takes control. Fear is only good when it gives you the strength and motivation to do what is needed to protect what is valuable to you.

Boredom – It is said that a man without a vision will perish. Boredom is the state of being without thoughts or participating in actions that keep one motivated. One must do more than just sit back on the lazy boy and watch sitcoms and realities shows. The mind and the body need constant quality stimulation. If boredom ever becomes a problem for you, refer to the chapter called Setting goals and making progress.

Negative Sex is a negative emotion that can be fatal to one's life, lively hood or family life. It is a force that causes one to lose control of one's faculties and pursue sex at a high level of desire and is often uncontrollable. Negative sex is extremely addictive and can lead one to reprioritize his or her values to satisfy this monster's needs. Like gambling and drug addiction it can control and manipulate one into neglecting their spouse and children for that orgasm that is strange, mysterious or risky.

Uncontrolled and or high risk sexual activities are the worse-case scenario. One can fall victim to some of life's biggest tragedies, like the contraction of AIDS, criminal arrest for solicitation or get into ones psyche and lead them to all sorts of evils like child molestation, rape, indecent exposure and so many more activities that could lead one down a road of disaster. The desire for sex can drain a bank account, cause divorce or lead one to jail or even death and illness. One must be wise and avoid this emotion as much as possible if not all together. It can lead to such a down fall that it must be controlled daily.......

As I stated earlier, misery loves company.

CHAPTER 5

THE ACTION AND
NEUTRAL EMOTIONS

Action emotions are essential for putting ones plans into existence and in motion. They have neither a positive or negative classification, when used by themselves or in combination with other action emotions. But, they are more powerful when used in combination with a positive or negative emotion. Without the frequent use of these emotions, obtaining ones goals in life can and will be extremely difficult.

Action emotions help one but at the same time challenge one to accomplish goals, see plans to their completion, complete life's tasks and maintain stability in one's life and endeavors. When there is a reward at the end of the tunnel like getting your way with the person you desire or accomplishing and important goal these emotions can create tasks that become a temporary labor of love. They are an essential part of your success formula. So I would advise you to use them in combination with only the positive emotions unless you are in protection mode and trying to fend off an enemy or negative presence.

Desire - Thought produces ideas and ideas produce desire. Desire is the emotion that causes one to want or wish for something. It can occupy all of your thoughts. It can be a driving force that motivates you to keep on keeping on. Desire can be positive or negative depending on its application. Used independently it is neutral. This emotion is not envy or jealousy and even though all three involve wanting something or someone, desire is in a class all by itself. Desire can set one on a course to accomplish their goals without the burden of having any of the negative emotions hanging around the neck, slowing one down and poisoning their efforts. Desire can be the foundation of something wonderfully successful. Desire is extremely powerful and can dictate a person's life and control them. So whenever desire is used it must be controlled to always send that individual in a positive direction.

Belief - Belief is the feeling of being sure of something. The act of knowing without necessarily seeing. Belief is an extremely important emotion. Without it almost all possibilities of success are limited and or eliminated. One must believe an idea in order to develop the desire needed to execute all available efforts to achieve one's mission or quest in this case. It gives one a set of guidelines or a foundation in a sense to base all thoughts pertaining to the subject of belief on.

Faith - Faith is a very strong belief or trust in someone or something, Faith is belief on steroids. Faith is like your new mind set's emotional foundation. Everything and anything is possible when faith is applied to it in a confident manner. Faith is what brave or crazy men use in war to gain the courage to fight. They apply faith in the belief that they will survive the next charge of their unit or the next push by the enemy. Faith has got to be what the sky diver, bungee jumper, mountain climber, tight rope walker or cliff diver uses to risk their lives for enjoyment. Personally life is too precious to me to risk it for fun but one must not judge people. We must maintain an open mind no matter what the circumstance is.

Determination - a quality that makes you continue trying to do or achieve something that is difficult. Determination is what one needs to exercise patience properly. Faith and Determination work hand in hand. Determination is the emotion that drives you to go farther when you are exhausted. It can give you that second wind you need to finish the race or journey. Imagine the distance runner that lives for marathons. They have mastered this emotion and put it into use every time they are in a race. Determination is that drive that tells them to not let demons into the mind that will cause them to stop running. They ignore the pain. Breathe in a manner to help their cardio endurance and push themselves all the way to the finish line.

Patience - the ability to wait for a long time without becoming annoyed or upset. Patience is a form of calmness and staying in control of your faculties while you wait for the thing that you seek. The best way to stay in control is to stay busy and by keeping your mind occupied on something that is worthwhile or potentially profitable. Ever hear the term patience is a virtue?

Bullshit!

Patience isn't a virtue, but the act of being patient is the virtue or positive action.

It's kind of like the knowledge is power phrase that some people believe. Knowledge is not power. Only the application of knowledge gives one the opportunity to gain power. Good things come to those who wait, is a lie. And when you are told, Jesus is going to give it to you, it is a way of stalling you from succeeding. It is true, the bible does contain the verse, "whatsoever you believe, and you will receive, when you pray, you shall have". But it doesn't say sit on your lazy ass till Jesus brings it to you. Don't fall for these tricks that will leave you unsuccessful. One must apply positive action while exercising patience to achieve success.

Confidence - Some people confuse this next emotion with its negative cousins, arrogance, conceit, egotism, etc. Confidence is good although it is possible to become over confident which can be very bad or put one in positions that could hurt or hinder the individual's progress... Ever heard the term too much of a good thing or anything is good when not used in excess. The way one becomes over confident is by inaccurately assessing ones skill sets and assets.

You must always have an accurate estimation of your strengths and weaknesses. When you misjudge these items you become over confident. The way to avoid being over confident is to figure out your confidence level. Then lower it below what you believe slightly. This is called being humble. Humility mixed with confidence is an unstoppable partnership.

Curiosity - the desire to learn or know more about something or someone. Curiosity is the emotion to deal with your internal and infinite learning curve. One must be willing to ask,"Who? Why? Where? What? When? What if? Etc"....

Curiosity is a very powerful emotion and as with any power one must use it with great wisdom. Ever hear the term curiosity killed the cat? You must have the wisdom to know when to just accept your assumptions and hypotheses about something and not test the situation because the answer may cost you more than you bargained for.

The phrase biting off more than you can chew comes to mind. Use this emotion as much as you can, safely. Exercise common sense and wisdom with every usage. Learn from your mistakes and move forward with the wisdom to never repeat what hasn't worked for you in the past without some improvement or adjustment to the original design. Curiosity combined with faith and belief will incubate and develop ideas into workable, sound and very achievable plans.

Sex - as a motivator sex is definitely an action emotion. It produces an increase in desires, commitment, motivation and determination. It will give one a surge of adrenaline and energy and can cause one to gain temporary confidence. A person will climb a mountain, sky dive, base-jump and risk their very life and become involved in different scenarios that could be considered life threatening for the possibility of sleeping with the person of their desire.

If one could harness this emotional power and be able to utilize it on command, one would have no problem accomplishing most obtainable tasks in life. Fences seem smaller, mountains become hills and speed becomes measured at a slower rate, they may try new foods, drink too much or a number of things they wouldn't normally do for the promise or opportunity to knock boots with a certain somebody.

One must be careful with this emotion because it can often turn into its negative sibling and have you sprung and strung out on someone.

Neutral emotions are non-empathetic and/or cold emotions. It is basically the lack of emotion. A coldness or non-feeling that usually comes when someone doesn't care anymore about a certain thing or person. A country hit by Jo Dee Messina called My Give A Damn's Busted comes to mind and kind of defines this concept completely. I really wanna care, I wanna feel something, Let me dig a little deeper.................

Naw, sorry, still nothing!

CHAPTER 6

PROFESSIONAL PSYCHOLOGY

Introduction

When I learn something new, I sometimes become angry or reckless for a time, but after a while the wisdom from the newly obtained knowledge kicks in and everything becomes controlled. Self-monitoring is an essential task one must do in order to make positive improvement in ones thinking and activities. You must study yourself, test yourself and set goals in your testing to stimulate your own growth and progress. Establishing time increments to achieve goals is extremely helpful to gage, follow and maintain progress. The product of this type of positive behavior is continuous self-improvement. Improvisation in this task and always trying new things will stimulate your mind to achieve progress, give you some entertainment and enjoyment as well as eliminate any boredom that may develop while doing this.

If there isn't a job, create it.

When I was in my early twenties, I told my wife at the time, that I wanted more from life than what I was doing. I was bored with college and delivering pizzas and working for a burger chain. I told her I was going to get a job that I could wear a suit and tie. I remember she barely had a reaction, but she wasn't negative about it. I didn't have a plan. All I possessed was the faith, belief, motivation, confidence and desire (***even***

though I had no reason to). I went to several employment agencies with a neatly typed resume. One problem I had no degree. Not realizing at the time that a degree wasn't mandatory to accomplish my goal, I added an imaginary degree on my resume.

I have never been a good liar and still haven't mastered that art form. I was also naive enough to think no would call my college and inquire if I had graduated or not. Well I had a few embarrassing moments because of this one lie on my resume and I deserved it for being dishonest. I even got an interview at a company I actually worked for as a consultant nearly twenty years later. The interview went extremely well. We broke for lunch. When I returned everyone's mood had changed to slightly angry and I was called out as the liar I was, and escorted from the premises. It is quite humorous that I worked for that company later in the exact same facility I was escorted out of.

At this point I realized my plan was obviously very flawed. I knew I was intelligent enough to do the work. I knew I had the personality to get the job. I felt beaten up, though. I temporarily gave up. About 4-5 months went by and I got a call from one of the employment agencies I had sent a resume too. This call was different. The agency was owned by a black lady. She had a defense contractor client. Due to the government requirements governed by affirmative action, they had to hire a number of minorities in order to be awarded government/military contracts. Sometimes the only way you can get a racist, homophobic or sexist person to not be that negative type of person is to show him or her they will not make money with that mindset. Money talks.

So because I was black and had a drafting background…I got the job. I went through a great deal of racism later because of the way I got my job, but I survived it and went on to become a Job Shopper. Sometimes you must invent the position you want. Invent the professional changes in your life.

Maintaining Positive Feelings of Accomplishment

It is essential to maintain positive feelings of accomplishment. To do so, you must set small goals for yourself, that add up to your ultimate goal or goals. Small goals are much easier to accomplish than larger ones. I know if I look at the big picture it can be a little daunting and overwhelming. Accomplish as many of these smaller goals as you can, and keep trying to succeed on the ones you fail at. Keep this up until you reach your ultimate goal. In the interim every time you succeed at a small goal it gives you a sense of accomplishment as well as gives you the excitement that you are that much closer to your ultimate goal.

Your desire to succeed and your faith in yourself will also be strengthened by these small goal accomplishments. Try smiling at someone every day that you know hates you for no logical reason. Their negative affliction is very contagious and you may find yourself thinking negative things about that person. None of this is good, so regardless of these feelings, keep on smiling. Force yourself to stay happy and positive. Sometimes it is better to just avoid these negative people until you can erase them from your life. Smile as often as possible whenever a smile is appropriate. Make fun of yourself. This will make you feel more positive about your faults and weaknesses as well as causes others to respect you for being the type that doesn't take himself too seriously.

Even though there will always be someone that doesn't like you, we must strive to be well liked. However, you must balance this by not caring what others think about you. Being well liked and appreciated is not an easy task, especially if you are a female, minority or a member of the LGBT community. Some people will never like you, admire you or show you any positive emotion.

Some people say "Oh, it's just the way they are" . Some will down play the disruptive attitude of this extremely negative and hateful person and they are as much your enemy as the one being negative.

Why? Because they want to deceive you. The phrase kill them with kindness is easier said than done. But we must try, when we do not have the opportunity to erase the negative influences out of our life.

The Perpetual Learning Curve

The perpetual learning curve is the way of describing how humans can learn for the rest of their lives. So feed it with information you want and need. Don't feed it with what the people programmers want you to think. We must block all of the negative and misinformation the people programmers bombard us with. Turn your cable television subscription off for good. We must become more intelligent every day. This will bring confidence to you in most conversation and in life in general. As always with any knowledge, once the brain has had ample time to process the information, one becomes wiser and has more foresight into the possible products and outcomes of more scenarios that one may experience in life.

Learning should always be enjoyable, so one will look forward to learning and feel the desire to not stop once they start. To do this one must start with knowledge that you can enjoy learning and can help you in your personal life and career. If these two factors are met, one can truly excel because the learning process takes a work ethic and this task should become a labor of love.

Negative Opinions and Influences

Negative Opinions and Influences should be dealt with in one way. Elimination.

In this country if cancer is discovered it can only be dealt with in two ways legally. By performing a biopsy and nuking it with chemo therapy. Negative influences are a cancer on your life and positive mental attitude. They need to be dealt with like this country deals with cancer—always.

Now don't get me wrong or take me out of context. All I am saying in reality is get the hell away from it. I have had the nasty experience of working in quite a few negative work environments. So being a Job Shopper at least, I always have an escape plan. Always keep your resume current and keep those automatic job ads coming in your email account. One job I had my blood pressure literally escalated and I learned what my Mother really meant when she said someone got on her nerves. I could physically feel nervous sensations in my arms. This was caused by so much negativity in the department I worked in. At times like this, one must ask one self, what is more important income, or health? I answer this question one way. I can get another job, but I can't get another life.

This is also possible in your personal life. Negative friends aren't your friends. They are a form of enemy, and will steal, kill and destroy goals and dreams that you have that they don't like or agree with. So any negative influence must be wiped out of your life, ASAP.

The Sub-Conscious Mind

The Sub-conscious mind can be your best friend or your worst enemy, depending on what you tell it to do. Most people don't realize that their sub-conscious mind is programmable and will control your conscious mind. The people programmers are aware of this and attack your sub conscious mind on a daily basis. You have an obligation to yourself to block this weapon of mental poison. The mind can only be either negative or positive at any given time. One must constantly reinforce both the conscious and subconscious to keep your mind positive. Think of a people programmer as a Shepherd and most people as sheep, literally. Anything the Shepherd says has to be right, even if it really doesn't make sense or violates the laws of physics.

Examples: Nine Eleven and the JFK assassination. The Shepherd's words are stronger than physics, the laws of nature and the laws of this country. The sheep are caught in a hypnotic trance and cannot hear the voice of reason. Your subconscious mind controls your impulses, thoughts and choices sometimes. It's that hunch that tells you not to do something or to do something. So if your subconscious mind has control over your conscious mind and you can program you subconscious then you have complete control over yourself.

Most people don't realize this fact and feed their subconscious mind with the negative thoughts of others and Television. In other words you give the advertisers and TV networks total control over you. Now that's scary, since all they see us as is a source of income and nothing else. You leave yourself thinking what fast food chains, insurance companies, household products and other corporations want you to think.

You are allowing them to control your impulses and change your habits to the habits they want you to have. Some people spend most of their waking hours, when not at work, watching this programming. Wow..., well that's exactly why they call it television "programming".

We go to bed watching and listening to our favorite TV shows. They have programming for our children so they can get the brain washing started early in the child's life so when they grow up they should be completely addicted to the way of life the corporations planned for them.

We must strive to break these mental chains and free our minds literally and the first step to mental freedom is stop watching too much TV.

Read a good book. Watch a biography. Take a walk or play a sport. Try going to sleep listening to something you want to learn or a good audio book. Choose your entertainment from the internet and find programs you have an interest in that are educational once in a while. It won't kill you to learn, but it will kill you to sit in front of that TV, smoking and getting obese eating the extremely unhealthy food that you see in most commercials. Just think, a clown holding a cheeseburger, has changed our way of life forever.

D. Byron Wiley

The Power of Laughter

People should always court laughter and find ways and things to make you laugh on a daily basis. Make a list of them and go about doing them today. Maintaining your positive attitude is by far your most important item every day. So when you need an immediate positive shot you have it. Comedy shows are always a good way to unwind after a rough week or day. A negative work environment is something that must be battled daily. You must leave work and give yourself more positive reinforcement than the amount of negative you received that day at work. The internet has comedy sites that are available anytime you need them. Also make friends that are silly and humorous. These people that are naturally funny. Search out these people that can make you laugh and keep them around you for a boost of laughter when your mood demands it.

I remember as children, we would always be sneaking to listen to Richard Pryor records. We wanted to laugh so bad it was worth potentially getting a woopin or possibly grounded for it. We need that strength of a desire to laugh as adults as well. When I am in my worst mood something as simple as a light hearted joke can send my mind and mood back on the right track again; the track to being positive. Remember, a healthy sense of humor is truly healthy.

The Straight Line Principle

Keep in mind, the closest distance between two points is a straight line. Always keep this in the back of your head. When you set your goals apply this principal. Anyone's ideas that can take you off your straight line to accomplishing your goal, you must ignore them at that moment and whenever they cause you this potential problem.

CHAPTER 7

PROFESSIONAL AMENITIES

Goal Setting........

At times in your life you need to re-evaluate and redefine if needed, your goal setting techniques. Once you have a sound plan, execute it. You do need to keep the basic formula though—

- Write down your chief aims.
- Set reasonable dates to accomplish them.
- Remember some progress is better than none. As long as you are moving forward there is no need to panic.
- Read them aloud with belief and faith that you can accomplish them, add the joy of you accomplishing your goals in your predetermined time frame and throw in some hope for future accomplishments once you reach these.
- Repeat this for everything you wish you accomplish or achieve.

In the Bible there is a verse in the Book of Mark that has stayed in my head my entire life. It is one of the very few Bible verses that I actually know and can recite. "Therefore I say unto you, whatsoever you desire, when you pray, believe that you receive them, and you shall have them." Again I am not religious anymore, but this is a strong statement and I know for a fact that it is real and works with efficiency.

The fact that I am an Engineering consultant is proof of this. I did not go to school for engineering. I went for Architectural Drafting as a major and

Broadcasting as a minor. I decided I wanted to do it. Put my faith in me and believed the words of **Mark 11:24**and accomplished something that almost no one would have believed I could if I told them prior.

My ex-wife looked at me with a blank expression. She had the wisdom not to be negative even though she had no belief in me obtaining this goal. She was happy I did accomplish it though. It started making our lives easier. This is the concept of Idea to reality. There is a technology called Stereo Lithography. It has been updated to be called the term **3-d printing**. I have literally thought of a part in my head. Created a scaled virtual model of it, exported the appropriate file and loaded the file into the 3-d printer. Hours later I am holding in my hand exactly what was once just energy…a figment of my imagination.

This is a perfect example of Mark 11:24 at work. The difference is one could say is I knew for a fact the 3-d printer would print the part I wanted. I had absolute faith it would work. One must feel the same way about oneself, when it comes to accomplishing the premeditated goals they have chosen. They must know for a fact it will work and don't let anyone tell you differently and live to tell about it…. just kidding. But you get the idea. Protect and respect your goals and dreams…if you don't no one will.

Rewarding Yourself

When you are writing down your goals and dates of accomplishment remember to create and plan a way of rewarding yourself for each goal or accomplishment. Never let your reward cost too much. It should never end up some sort of Pyrrhic victory.

It needs to be more of a symbolic reward, to keep you positive and help you maintain good spirits about accomplishing your task. One should make a list every now and then, because our interests tend to change at times in our life. A list of some things that you enjoy, that are not very expensive, are entertaining and or fun, bring a benefit to your life and cause you to look forward to them. Anytime you accomplish a goal or plan choose a reward and enjoy yourself.

Getting started in your industry

Proper marketing is the key to any successful venture. Same thing in obtaining any job. The Shopper must write or have someone else write a solid resume, emphasizing the shopper's skills, accolades and accomplishments in a very professional manner. Once this is completed the resume needs to be electronically distributed to the job shops (Contractor Employment Agencies). The resume also should be uploaded on websites like monster. com, Contract Weekly, Dice, etc.

Your Inner Circle

People in your inner circle need to think like you do. This is critical to your success. You need people that have similar opinions and preferences, professional as well as personal. Also they need to contain certain strengths and skill sets that you do not have but will complement your efforts. They need to share your sense of humor and appreciate the type of comedians and comedies that you do. Common hobbies wouldn't hurt either. They must share your passions. You must be able to get along with them and keep positive attitudes between you. They need to be someone you can confide in comfortably without feeling negative vibes. They need to be mentally stable and not all over the place emotionally. They need to be the same personality every time they come in contact with you.

They need to be people you have a natural respect for and you need to be the same with them. Both must feel a common empathy with each other and have the compassion to never intentionally betray one another.

Once you decide you want this person in your inner circle, decide what their role will be in your life and what you will be to them. Study them. Learn their strengths and weaknesses. Take mental notes on how they respond in certain situations. Watch and learn their body language. Anybody that is a candidate for your inner circle must live by the two way street principle. If they do not, the selfish party needs to be left alone until they understand the two way street principal.

What this principal is, is understanding what is selfish and what is not. It's a partnership of sorts. Both parties look out for each other. Both help each other. Both appreciate each other. Both share wisdom with each other; maintain a balance of mutual benefits and understanding. Anticipate each other's needs before they become a need and acting on the hunches to eliminate the need. Be honest to a point. Never let your need to be honest weigh more than the relationship. Some things are better off unsaid and/or forgotten about. If intimacy, romance or sexual activities develop, embrace them as long as they have no negative by products.

Choosing a mate

When choosing a love interest, preferably from your inner circle one should measure three emotions for you within the person. All three need to be strong or all this person should be to you is a friend if you find yourself drawn to them intimately. Compassion, empathy and respect. Ask yourself six questions and if all the answers are yes, this person is a very good candidate for a mate.

- Can you say honestly that you feel a need to take care of them?
- Do you feel they want to be there for you and take care of you?
- Do you want to feel what they feel emotionally?
- Do you think they want to feel what you feel emotionally?
- Last but not least do you respect them?
- Would you say they respect you?

If all of these questions can be answered with a yes, again this is a great candidate for a mate.

I once dated a lady and she was very warm, very intimate and seemed to be very caring, however after spending the night with her, I left her apartment feeling emotionally slimy. I could not figure out why. Then I asked myself the six questions I mentioned earlier and we didn't get all six yes answers. Question number one and two were both yes. Question number three was yes. Question number 4 was no. Question 5 was yes and question number six was and unconscious no.

If you make plans and goals in your life, in order to achieve them you must surround yourself by like-minded people. She and I have two different minds and she is also a sheep.

Sheep and Free Thinkers inherently clash sooner or later, because one is close minded and one is open-minded. Polar opposites. She later told me she used compassion at times to manipulate people. And for those of you that believe opposites attract, I would hope I have changed your mind.

Yes men and No men.

Keep yes men and no men second tier. They have very good uses that are extremely positive to you. When dealing with an enemy you need to send your no man. A person that needs undue attention you send your yes man. Never let these two speak on any thing that matters in your inner circle. The no man is a hater point blank and the yes man is an ass kisser. Neither one do you want or need near you. Guilty by association. I will speak more on the yes men and no men in Chapter 16: Offensive Strategies.

See Your Dream Daily

Experience your dream before you achieve it. In order to stay positive and focused on your goals, you must place in your mind the physical things that represent the success you want to achieve. Go out to the type of neighborhoods you want to live in and study the types of homes you want to live in. Take some trips to car lots and study the types of vehicles you want to drive. Study the type business your want and befriend people in that business and last but not least your imagination must come into play. You must see the amount of money you want. Imagine it in your hand. Imagine your bank statement bottom line. Whatever you need to do to imagine this money daily, do so.

The hand shake

Handshakes have come a long way from the time when they were only a way of greeting someone, saying goodbye or a gesture of agreement. They have evolved into a science of their own. They can mean different things.

I will start with the basic shake. Two vertical hands with the squeeze equal on both sides. This is a sign of equality and mutual respect. If one person turns their palm upwards they are giving a sign of submission. On the other hand if you turn your palm downward you are showing dominance.

I often shake a ladies hand palm up at times to cause her to make her comfortable with me and not feel like I am going to dominate her. If someone turns your hand up as they turn theirs downward and you do not like this try placing your other hand over theirs and this shows that you have taken the dominance back.

Some other power handshakes are reaching with the other hand for their elbow and to grab the other person's shoulder with the free hand. I would not suggest using these power handshakes unless you are aware of the consequences and you know the personality of the person you are shaking with. Oh and three to five pumps are a good average that should work.

As one walks in the footsteps of the Job Shopper, he or she must keep the straight line principle in mind. The closest distance between two points is a straight line. You are at one end of the line when you set a goal. The opposite end of the line is representative of you accomplishing your goal. Never let anything or anybody get you to walk off your lines or paths to your goals being accomplished. Anybody that knowingly tries is your enemy to a certain extent. So pay attention. Listen, observe and remember, always.

CHAPTER 8

INCOME, OUTGO, IFCOME AND IFGO

Imagine a current of water, or if you are into electronics the flow of electricity. I tend to see money flow in a similar manner that I call 3-d imagination. I see how I have over spent at times in the past and I understand how to actually save money. I am also aware of how to spend less as well, which corporate marketing has borrowed the word save to represent spending less. Money flows into your possession and out of your possession, sometimes by your choice and sometimes beyond your control.

Imagine a shipping port. Most people forget they actually run the port for the most part. Life has a way of getting 24/7 access to your imports and exports. Most often, if you don't earn a six figure income there is usually never enough incoming traffic through your imports.

Since most people only focus on income I will start there. I realized from dealing with money over the years and seeing far more go out than come in at times in my life, I knew I always need to be concerned.

Income - is the acceptance of wages and salaries also known as your pay check, Income can come from other means such as investment profits, interests payments from money lent out, rent payments from rental housing and the sale of items created

Outgo on the other hand is the exact opposite of income, hence the name out-go. Outgo is not your friend. Outgo is household bills, car payments, insurance payments, basically anytime money is spent for any reason it goes in this category.

In my opinion, income needs to be at least if not more, twice as much as the outgo.

These next two are basically all in our minds, because once they become real, they become the previous two directions of money flow.

Ifcome is a word that I used to hear older people use often when I was a child. Like Outgo it is not a real word, but it does have meaning. Ifcome is that money that is promised to you.

It could be a refund that is suppose to come in the mail. It's the imaginary money that people often attempt to use as collateral when attempting to borrow money. I remember being in my father's store when I was a child and hearing his friends use this term. The conversation would go a little like this. Black man, can you let a brother hold a few bucks. The most likely response is, "when would the person get the money back". This is the point when Ifcome would be brought up as collateral. When so-n-so gets their pay check, they said they are going to give me the money they owe me. In my experience of dealing with black people is, Ifcome usually means no come, so it is not a good idea to loan money unless you know for a fact a person is trustworthy, but if you do, forget about it and pretend it's a gift in your mind. Never acknowledge this feeling verbally to anyone. This will eliminate potential negative feelings developing between you and the person borrowing money. I have seen people fight people that have loaned them money. Hell of a way to show appreciation for the favor. Usually they just pretend you never loaned it to them and sometime change the subject or get irritable when the subject is brought up of the loan.

Ifgo, is something that only a chronic worrier tends to focus on. I believe in thought that it isn't an issue or problem until it becomes one. If you don't know for a fact a bill or debt needs to be paid then it should not be a concern until you are notified that it is. It would not hurt to prepare for outgo. Preparation and proper planning are never a bad thing. Worse case, scenario, you may have extra money that you set aside for Ifgo that could be used for something else that is needed or maybe even wanted..

Good Investments are tricky to see and find. They are the best kept secrets. No one wants someone to beat them to the finish line. Most people aren't forthcoming with good investment information unless they want to make money with you or swindle you out of some money. One must read between the lines. One must learn to listen to what is not being said. People have a tendency to tell you almost anything you want to know if you listen long enough with an open non-judgmental mind. One must learn to ask questions that hide the question they are actually asking. Sometimes if one doesn't know what you are looking for they will show you what you want to see or know in this case without realizing they are giving in to your curiosity.

Good investments sometimes go unnoticed. They seem to hide in plain sight. Other times there is someone there blinding you with negative conversation and reasons why you can't, shouldn't or won't.

Bad Investments are easy to find. So don't go looking for them. They have the ability to find you. They will often come to you in the form of a friend and old acquaintance, relative or a lover. I happen to personally know a very successful man that has shown me compassion and listened to me at times. He once told me to get a business package together and let him see it. He also offered to help me by giving me some equipment to restart my recording studio. I declined the equipment because I was traveling at the time due to Job Shopping and had no safe place to use it or store it.

About a year or so later, I was approached by an individual that was as motivated as I was and am. To this day I don't know for a fact if he is a good person or bad, but listening to him cost me a very valuable friend. He introduced me to someone that had a movie concept. Together we put together an investment business plan. I looked it over but having barely any experience or knowledge in the financing of a movie, I could not see the inflated numbers that were inserted into each financial statement or explanation. They were asking for a number that was at least 5 times what was needed. Being naive I sent the package to my successful friend.

Let's put it this way, we haven't spoken since. What did me in was my blind desire, artificial confidence, lack of educated knowledge of what I was asking my friend to do financially and poor planning. Most important of all, I did not know who I was putting myself in business with. All factors that added up to a potential bad investment for anyone that came in contact with us.

I have always tried to do business with a mindset that everyone involved should benefit. I was guilty of trusting the wrong people. Sometimes one can get you to make a bad investment because of your emotions. When it comes to money there is no productive reason to bring emotion into it. Emotion's will cloud your judgment, influence negatively and blind you from making wise decisions. One's financial safety is a priority, if one plans to be successful. One must be rounded, yet not closed minded. He or she should constantly be looking for ways to improve his or her income and increase their net worth. One must be quick to listen and slow to speak. One must be quick to watch and not move forward with any investment until they have the essential amount of knowledge and wisdom to proceed confidently. Everybody and their brother has an investment for you. My friend has every reason to not trust me and or not speak to me again and I don't hold that against him.

Generosity is a compassionate gesture that one must not engage in without the wisdom to know the person they have compassion for. Generosity should not even be considered when dealing with someone. One must show themselves worthy of your generosity prior to you being generous to them. Ask any celebrity about fake friends. These fly by night leeches that cling to people that let them like glue. Jay Z in the record "Holy Grail" speaks about this referencing the youngest heavyweight champion of all time, Iron Mike Tyson. Mike Tyson earned 35 million in one night and everybody deserted him when they couldn't get any more of his favors or thought he was broke. I myself once had an entourage of over twenty people at the high point of HHN Records. I haven't heard from any of those people in years and I am sitting here alone writing this book.

CHAPTER 9

FAMILY LIFE

As soon as we hit the work force in life, one desire most people have is to constantly increase their income. Whether personal, family, investments etc. it is on everyone's mind. I did a little better than 2.5 times my first salary when I made the switch from my first direct job and an entered the contract world. Which was low, but I didn't know that then. A year later it was four times my original salary. Presently I am earning approximately more than eight times the amount of my first engineering job.

I remember back when I did my exit interview of my first engineering position, the man that opened the engineering software door for me told me, "You are gonna make a lot of money" Shook my hand, walked off and I never saw him again.

For a Shopper, having a spouse and family is always a work in progress. They say absence makes the heart fonder, but being miles away from your spouse most of the time is taking it to the extreme. You can't be a job shopper without traveling most of the time. There are however, areas of the country where a Shopper can just stay in one area.

I call this Corridor shopping. These types of work assignments are perfect for a Shopper if they have a family. Unfortunately these areas or job pockets can have one or two major corporations in that area have massive layoffs and send an employment tsunami through the area. The Shopper is usually the first one to get laid off in these times. This causes the Shopper to hit the road again, in order to secure an employment contract. Having someone there that misses you and is waiting for you at the door when you come home off the road, can be an extremely wonderful thing at a time like that.

Having a family forces one to budget and spend money with wisdom, due to home's financial responsibilities. The Shopper has a great deal of freedom when on the road. So another person in the same boat with him or her keeps them from living a double life, usually. Sometimes life's distractions can "distract". Literally. I will go into depth about life's distractions in the next couple chapters.

A spouse that will run the enterprise from home effectively can be a good thing. Although I would use great caution and wisdom before engaging in this type of venture with your spouse. I just said it could, be a good thing. Someone else with a vested interest in the enterprise is the perfect person to discuss potential contract logistics with. Someone to bounce topics of discussion off of like... What is the contract location? How much gas would it take to get there? Is the car good for that distance? Is a rental car worth it? How much does the contract pay? Is there Per Diem? Will there be overtime? What shift is it? Is there affordable temporary housing in the area? What is the technical level of difficulty of the job? This communication and support structure would do two things - Assist the shopper and take some of the stress off of them as well as keep an open line and a constant line of communication with the spouse. This communication is essential in keeping a relationship positive when traveling to a job.

Job shopping is a business and needs to be approached and looked at in this manner. There is an initial investment as with any business. A period of time, when no income is made. (Usually 2-6 weeks, but normally and in most cases, 2 weeks). One should keep all receipts for meals, gas and motel expenses. A scanner would come in handy for filing of these documents. So this is a job and business that your spouse can participate in. Also, they can always come along at times to eliminate the loneliness of the road.

A fringe benefit of being a shopper is being able to afford a few luxuries for your family. That is always nice. Vacations, private schools, upper middle class homes, and a quality of life that is very, let's just say, you may not get rich, but you still can have a very comfortable life.

Life can seem like it passes you by, since a good portion of the family milestones are missed, due to the time away from the family. This is when the marriage and the family has to be supported by positive emotions and energies in order to stay strong. This is also when negative people tend to start false rumors and others approach with selfish motives. The isolation from family can attract negative emotions as well, such as loneliness and a feeling of emotional neglect. Sometimes this may cause one to weaken and decide to see someone else on the side, due to their significant other not being available to them romantically and or sexually.

This brings me to the word infidelity, which in my opinion is the most destructive enemy to any family and to the institution of marriage. This is not because of the act of infidelity, but is because of how the other spouse reacts to it.

Infidelity has many negative emotions as companions. When this term is defined and broken down it is easy to determine why divorce rates are so high in this country. The term infidelity destroys more families possibly, than any other cause. The term infidelity is accompanied by selfishness, greed, revenge, jealousy, betrayal, anger and hate. The companions of infidelity separate children from parents and forever change a child's life in a very negative manner.

Some parents carry infidelity with them like it's a "get a new spouse card" if they decide they hate the present one that much for what they can or could do. There always seem to be a friend that yells, "Leave them", whenever the marriage hits a rough patch to make matters worse.

Did the act of infidelity hurt the children's life in reality? No. The reaction of the spouse hurts the children in reality. A child needs both parents at home with a unified front dedicated to raising their offspring as best possible.

I am not even remotely sure why wedding vows are still in the marriage ceremony. Isn't this a waste of time with most likely both parties carrying the "get a new spouse card" in their back pocket? The vows have no value and the children's needs come second to the parents wants. That's not a parent I would want to raise me if I was still a child. I would want one that would put the needs of the family above the wants of themselves.

I am a bit of a hypocrite here. I never carried the "get a new spouse card" because I never planned on leaving my wife. We had plans for five children and I wanted every last one of them. I was blessed with a son, and I also had a daughter by a relationship prior to my marriage.

Anyway it's a shame that a hurt parent would allow their demons to destroy what they built for their child and sentence them to an existence of confusion. If the children are our futures then why aren't they the driving motivation for a marriage to succeed if children are always better off with two good parents rather than one good one?

Please don't misunderstand. I am not condoning staying in a bad marriage. That may not be wise at all for anyone involved. I am just saying the marriage has to constantly evolve with the child's changing needs and the effect society has on the family unit in order to raise the child in the best manner possible. This is the most important thing to consider as a parent. The child's interest comes first. They didn't ask to be here. You brought them into this world. The child's mental health should be a main focus of a marriage, not catering to a selfish parents own wants and feelings. Change your thinking and throw your "get a new spouse card" away, for your child's sake. It's not too much to ask.

Divorce is a financial field day for courts and lawyers. Let's think about this for a moment. Lawyers get paid by the hour or they get a 30% commission in most cases. Courts aren't there for free. There are always court costs.

Let's say a family is living a modest upper middle class life. Let's say the mother is a stay at home Mom and the father is a lower level director in a major corporation. They have three children ages 2, 8, 12. Let's say the husband has an affair with a co-worker. It was a drunken fluke. There are no emotions and it was just physical. He is completely in love with his wife. Let's say he feels much remorse and guilt. Yes ladies, this is a possibility. Love is a separate emotion than any one of the three sex emotions. One can be completely in love with someone and can still be seduced by another person.

It's not all the cheater's fault. Men were created to do one thing and that is to reproduce, meanwhile eating, breathing, defecating waste and sleeping along the way. Anything else in this life, man or woman invented. Most likely if he was weak enough to get seduced in the first place his wife is most likely not having enough sex with him and he has a lot of built up sexual tension and other women can sense this. It is a scientific fact that there are things a man's body does that are hard wired and we do it without thinking or realizing it. These twitches, movements, blinks, responses all reveal what we are feeling or thinking. To any woman that can recognize these things and is aware of our weaknesses in this manner, men are sitting ducks to be seduced in any manner these women choose.

So if you are someone's wife or girlfriend, quit using sex as a weapon. It will backfire on you. Seduce him regularly in order to keep your man happy. Bring your inner freak out for them. As I said previously, there must be compassion, empathy and respect in the relationship always and you must be his best friend, you must be concerned for his health and you must make love to him whenever it is not an inconvenience.

OK, let me get back on subject. Let's say they have a $250,000.00 house with only $100,000 in equity, three vehicles, valued at $80,000.00 total. Misc. household assets of $105,000.00. and about $130,000.00 in investments and savings. Let's say the wife files for divorce. The court orders a 50/50 split of assets and the house should be sold along with liquidation of the family's investments to help pay off debt, lawyers and court cost and the rest split between the couple.

Now both parents must get their own places and buy new furnishings that they lost in the divorce. Both houses must be set up so that the children have a comfortable life, both places, and the value of both added together in most cases will be less than the house that was sold and both parents may have to rent for a while. The children must shuffle back and forth between two residences and literally be forced to live two lives. Not to mention, since both parents must pay for two separate homes and two different lives think about how the children are affected financially. Paying for college will be more difficult for the parents. Vacations will be rarer. Double household expenses forces both parents to consider remarriage and force their children to possibly live with a stranger that they do not know and do not care for and may despise. Or they could despise their new step children. The children could inherit a step parent that is a child molester or other type of abuser..

Divorces can wreak havoc on anyone affected by it. Businesses can be ruined. Children's inheritance can be eaten up in legal fees and court costs. At the end of the day, is divorce all it's cracked up to be? As I said in the beginning, it's a field day for lawyers and the courts and destroys children emotionally. The legal system gets free money and the family has to rebuild everything. All because one parent thought that their feelings were more important than their children's needs and wants and pulls their "get a new spouse card" out of their back pocket and displays it with force and passion.

Again, I am not saying stay in a bad marriage. If your spouse is abusing you, a split is in the better good of all. The children do not need to see their mother or father abused. In today's society divorce is looked at as the thing to do whenever a marriage hit's a rough patch; the ultimate solution. However, is divorce the answer though? Why give your hard earned money away to someone that doesn't deserve it. That money would be better spent on your children's future, in my opinion. I have met couples in the past few years that have open relationships and stay together even after the children move out and they are still in love.

Now religious people are freaking out about what I am writing I am sure, however I would rather be with my spouse of many years, be in love with her and have all my money in my old age than be alone and only have, less than half the money I should have. Pray on that.

CHAPTER 10

NEGATIVE EFFECTS OF CULTURE AND ENVIRONMENT

Family and friends, for various reasons, will use negative advice to get one to scrap your ideas to succeed in life. I believe a great deal of it boils down to the negative emotions of envy, jealousy, hatred and insecurity. Sometimes people can never financially recover from the devastation that these family members and friends make on their lives with their negative concepts and advice. Instead of working together for a common good, they would rather place bets that you will fail, cheer and applaud your failure and ridicule you if you have the courage to try it again. I have noticed that some people make fun of cultures that stick together and help each other as a group to succeed and get ahead in their lives. "There is like ten of them in one apartment".

I know most landlords won't go for that, but this is intelligent thinking none the less. I feel competition is good and healthy, but when it comes to life people should help each other, in a perfect world. Too bad we don't live in one. One must pick and choose very cautiously any one they want to help. Appreciation is not a trait most people carry with them or display very often except prior to getting what they want. Once they get what they want, one is discarded as if the help never came.

A wise man once said, the world could cease to exist if all compassion was eliminated. History has shown how some empires and countries show little compassion for smaller less powerful countries and do horrible things to them physically and financially. In this country genocide for the most part was committed on the natural natives of this land in order to acquire the land. I remember as a child we were brain washed into believing that the natives were the bad guys, when they were actually the victims. So when people see this in movies, and on the news, they are programmed to think in this manner. Some people that happen to be evil and wealthy, want us to be crabs in a barrel, so they can scoop up all the money while we are distracted fighting amongst ourselves over the most trivial of things, like politics, religion, sports and the negative emotions. They want us to get divorced. They want our children to grow up ill prepared for life's challenges. They want us to believe exactly what they tell us or we are considered crazy or conspiracy theorist because some people choose to think with their own minds. (Like 9 11 and the Magic bullet). They want us to be sheep and not question anything, just do as we are told. That constitutes a closed mind and a closed mind is stagnated indefinitely, because people that have closed minds lack the ability to think for themselves. A closed mind cannot grow.

Some of the worst advice I have ever gotten has come from friends and relatives. Again I feel that because of the philosophies of Willie Lynch, Black people (being one myself) are the extreme, as far as giving negative advisement towards a positive venture. I was once advised I should go to a business meeting without a business plan, without a presentation and without my ducks in a row and the individual giving the advice was serious, just because I personally knew the millionaire I was meeting with. The millionaire told me to put together a business plan when I showed up without one.

Shame on me—

I always wondered why some Black people have separated themselves from the majority of Black people when they started developing a sound financial foundation. These people were always called or referred to as stuck up. I have a tendency to call them wise, now that I understand what is really going on. The term "crabs in a barrel" rings true. No one seems to want to see anyone rise before them. The Golden Rule was taught to us as children, but somehow it must have been written in an alien language because no one understands it anymore or pays any attention to its moral qualities.

Any friend or blood relative I told I was going to be a Job Shopper threw up all kinds of hurdles and negative motivation to try and change my mind. It's not a regular job. It's only temporary. They can lay you off without notice. You have no job security. You don't get benefits. You are going to have to live out of a motel. You are too far from home. What about your son? You can't be dragging him all over the country.

Most of my family feels that just because I earn a certain level income I should spend more, which is the absolute worst advice that could be given. I had one relative tell me you should get a BMW. I said why do I want a payment that large? They confidently said you can afford it. Now they knew full well that job shopping is temporary work and there would be times I would not be working and that payment and car insurance would still be due every month. Now I look back on it and it is in my opinion that they wanted me to bite off more than I could chew so I could fall off, fail…maybe get the Beemer repossessed. Being a contractor I don't want any debt at all.

Competing with society's view point of how much your house should be worth, what kind of car you drive etc. is not wise. One must isolate their financial thoughts from outside ears. I have given up TV for the most part because it fills ones head with so much negative malarkey. I strive to keep my mind pure and full of positivity so that I constantly make positive progress even if it's only a small amount at a time.

Sub Cultures and the Art of Neutrality—

The art of staying neutral is something that everyone should perfect. I have fallen victim to the lures of sub-cultures myself. One must be a fly on the wall and watch and learn, but sometimes becoming a part of a really cool sub culture may not be in your best interest, so be careful. While writing this book, I realized one beautiful summer morning that it was much easier for me to write at the moment, the chapters on negative emotions and concepts and harder to write about positive ones.

This caused me to think in depth about this phenomenon of my mind. I read many positive mental attitude books and documents as a young adult and I made the assumption that because I thought I had a positive mind, I did.

I was imaginative, determined, had faith and confidence and was always trying to bring some new entrepreneurial type of business concept to financial success and maturity. I was also by contrast, selfish, manipulative and dishonest when I shouldn't be or had no logical reason to be.

However, in writing this manuscript, I realized obviously I knew more about the negatives than the positives. So does this mean I have a negative mind? I believe it says I had sub consciously taken in more negative concepts and feelings than positive. This led me to conclude the people I chose to be around me and the concepts I was learning, were laced with negative components that mostly went by unnoticed to me.

I believe the culture of Hip Hop and the philosophies of Willie Lynch letter in combination caused this to happen to me. The philosophies of Willie Lynch letter sent extreme negative emotions, concepts and self-hatred through black families during the time in the history of this country, when Black People were legally considered livestock, exactly like a farm animal. In this country, this has affected black families negatively for hundreds of years. It taught us to be perpetually negative. Perpetually self-hateful and literally despising who we are as a people.

It taught us to shun our own history as if it was the institution of slavery itself. If you ask the average black person where Timbuktu is and what it means to them, they would not have a clue, nor would they care. Other nationalities are proud of their ancestry in this country. French are proud of Paris, the British are proud of London, the Spanish of Madrid, Japanese of Tokyo the Italians of Rome, etc. Most Black people don't know they are possibly Hausa, Mandingo, Asante, Ibo or a mixture of them, and again nor do they care.

The crazy thing is, it would surprise and shock most people of this country that if it weren't for the negative institution of American Slavery, most descendants of slaves would be Islamic, not Christian. That was one of the things taken away from the slave in order to cause them to believe they were less than human.

Anyway, I apologize for going off subject, but it gave a little more in-depth understanding of just how powerful the philosophies of Willie Lynch letter were and are. So based on that fact; most things and habits black people have and create in this country are copied redundantly and modified by other cultures and races.

All you have to do to see or hear this phenomenon is turn on your TV today and hear Black sayings that were once only heard in the "Hood" and now they are a part of most major corporations' advertising campaigns and slogans. I am sure our entire society has been touched by these negative philosophies of Mr. Lynch deeply. I am sure that racial lines have not slowed down this torpedo as it speeds through the minds of people that come in contact with it. The chickens, have come home to roost.

The Battle Rap—

Hip Hop, for example, has a whole section or sub culture that is entirely based on saying negative things about one another in and out of the culture. Sometimes the worst things said can be the most popular.

Everyone strives to state the sickest rhymes. It's called battle rapping and this lifestyle can also be heard in diss records. I myself wrote and performed a verse on a record for HHN Records that encompassed this style of rapping. I was so caught up in Hip Hop that I even started smoking blunt cigars.

Craziest thing ever is I can read and on every box I bought it stated that the product will cause heart disease, well guess what? Now I have congestive heart failure or CHF. I was nicknamed Chief and it wasn't because I am a CEO.

I should of been the fly on the wall on that one and it's too late now. It is what it is. I must deal with the circumstances as positively as I can. It's a matter of life or death. Literally. Heavy D, an extremely talented gentleman passed away some time ago. He is often seen in promotional photo's with a signature cigar. He suffered from heart disease. Congestive heart disease sufferers are often prescribed blood thinners to attempt to lower the risk of clotting. On December 27, 2011 an autopsy report was released. The document stated that the artist's cause of death was a pulmonary embolism. It had broken off from a deep vein thrombosis in his leg. The blood clot most likely formed during a long flight. The artist was reported to have just returned from performing in Cardiff, Wales at a tribute to Michael Jackson. So, now I have to make all sorts of changes in my life just to stay healthy. Take it from me, if it says it will kill you, it probably will.

No one is emotionally made of steel; however some of these rappers appear to be. The culture of hip hop is homo-phobic and very negatively critical to others in different cultures and sub cultures. There is a great deal of hatred in the sub cultures of hip hop. If you break down the rap battle and the diss record one can easily see the philosophies of the character of Willie Lynch are deeply entrenched in most of the culture. Remember the whole East West thing, Bad Boy vs. Death Row, Tupac vs. Biggie, Dre vs. Eazy, Naz vs. Jay Z, and L.L. vs. Can I Bus.

So many rappers have experienced violence. Some are dead now and others may die in the future, due to this violent subconscious programming that all members of the Hip Hop Culture have embraced at some time in their lives. Dre Day and Hit em Up are two of my favorite records to this day. Since records are listened to over and over again till they are memorized one must admit to one's self that they are programming their subconscious to think in the manner of the record.

CHAPTER 11

EXTRA-CURRICULAR ACTIVITIES

The Dual life possibility

Sometimes one's imagination can run wild when you get some freedom that wasn't expected. Keeping your priorities in order and staying on your path to your goals must be your driving factors when an unexpected, unlimited amount of freedom comes your way. It would be quite easy to live a double life. Your life at home with your spouse and family versus your life on the road as a job shopper. Personalities, environment, the amount of entertaining things to do can all factor into the phenomenon that can develop from having a second life. This phenomenon could be negative or positive, or even neutral. It is what each individual makes of it.

The Dating Scene

When the shopper is on the road traveling, the lure of romance, intimacy and or sex can motivate the shopper to do things that may not be the normal routine or habits. One often needs to accommodate for the need to eliminate the loneliness that comes from being on the road and most likely not knowing anyone in the area of the job site and, the physical needs and desires for sex. This is true whether the person is single, has a romantic friend, is engaged, married, divorced or widowed. I suggest if you are in a closed and committed relationship, to find ways of communicating and seeing your significant other as often as possible, without over doing it.

One should go home and spend quality time with them, call when needed, write emails, teleconference or whatever means is affordable and available. This will be sufficient for the needs of your relationship. This is essential to keeping your personal life successful as well as your professional life.

Since you only do the professional part to enhance the personal, you can understand how important it is to maintaining the positive attitude needed to maintain the progress one has made and continue in the that pattern you have created for yourself. If one does not do this they will be subject to the pitfalls of the distractions of negative seducers.

There are many types of seducers and just because it is usually defined as something sexual this concept has a far broader range than that. Self-control and maturity are the keys to this principle.

I recall a record by, Bell Biv Devoe, called "Poison". Just because someone has the physical attributes that you desire does not mean you should let your guard down and allow this person to seduce you and possibly side track you or worse destroy you. One must look beyond the physical characteristics. I know that is easier said than done, but one can accomplish this through repetitious and redundant efforts to succeed.

One must learn to ask the right questions to determine who they are dealing with. There are all kinds of people that one must be concerned about. I will name and describe four later in this section. Please keep in mind that being a male myself I tend to use the feminine terms as a significant other so if I say female or women, this can also be applied by women for men. Consider this non-gender.

Some women tend to use men and will have a tendency to target a job shopper because they have somehow determined that he can do things for her and not sweat it that some men can't or won't. Throw your chivalry hat in the trash can.

One must be open minded with each woman he meets because every women has chosen different preferences in her life. Even though some things are hard wired in people there are always differences. So one must not judge and just observe enough to determine what is in store for you being with that person and make wise decisions about dealing with them.

Some women feel that they are entitled to supplement their entertainment budget; to enjoy time in their life without having to pay for anything, by preying on generous, compassionate men that fall in love easily

These women don't possess compassion for these men. They could care less how much negativity they cause these men. They have tunnel vision and can only see their wants, desires and needs and if this particular guy is not playing ball there are several more waiting in line that will. This is a nightmare for the monogamous, insecure person. They succumb to this form of sadistic seduction because of the fear of heart break or being alone. Once these people smell that scent coming from you, you will become easy prey. So if any woman or man causes you to feel this, you must have the self-control to walk away and never look back. This person will only use you and that is not what you are seeking. Beware these women; unless this is what you like........I did warn you though.....

All four of the following women tend to try to manipulate and control men. They are all very demanding and tend to adore the use of double standards. There is no such thing as fairness with these women. It's their way or the highway in a lot of cases. They will always use sex and any other thing they determine you desire to manipulate you or as the saying goes, as a weapon. Now, two aren't too bad and depending on what you want in a significant other may actually be good for you if you are the monogamous and or insecure type. Women can apply these same traits to men to determine if they are the male version of these personas.

"The Daddy's Girl" versus "The Church Girl"

Both of these ladies are the quote, unquote, white picket fence and dream house, family type of women. Both will be wonderful wife types, however, remember that most of the time, both carry the "get a new spouse card" if he cheats or develops negatives that tend to have a negative effect on "her" ideal life. So keep in mind, if you want and choose or have chosen this type of lady, one must be good to them or they will make you pay dearly later, financially, emotionally or both. So understand their definition of betrayal and forget yours, because only theirs has power in the laws of the relationship. She could care less what you think in this case.

The cool thing about both of these women is they usually only focus on one guy. One that can and will give her the stability she needs, desires and wants. Now stability means two different things to these women. The Daddy's Girl obviously wants to find her father's type in a husband or lover because she admires the relationship her Mother has with her Father and wants to duplicate this type of household in her life. So she will seek out these men and make herself available to date them. She usually expects him to open doors, pay for almost all of their dates entirely and treat her like a princess. She will constantly use romance or the lack of, to stimulate her target into falling in love, so she can control him through his emotions and emotional weaknesses. The beautiful thing about these women is if they fall for you, she will do her best to be your ideal lover as long as you keep her happy in the relationship. When the man fails to do so she will take things away like a mother punishing her child. Ever heard a man say his wife has him in the dog house?

Well, if he wore the pants in his family and relationship this can never happen. A man that perfects the constant seduction of his wife will be forever happy with her.

The Church Girl is a lot like Daddy's Girl, except as the title says the institution of church changes her. She will not let you know her dirty thoughts as a Daddy's Girl will. She may not go to church frequently but still has the mentality of one that does. She will let you try to seduce her and seemingly never give in, when the Daddy's Girl will be opposite.

A Daddy's Girl will talk about the dirty things in her mind but doesn't want you focused on them all the time. The Church Girl is very grounded and will not venture out of the fenced in yard in her head. She will come across uptight and will only date men with her religious beliefs or the willingness to compromise or convert to her way of worshipping God, whereas a Daddy's Girl wants to be loved by a guy that thinks like her Dad.

They will both leave you eventually if they feel that their investment in your relationship is not leading to marriage or a long term committed relationship. So when you date these women you are on the clock. Keep in mind, I don't care how good your skills are, they will choose a committed life and relationship over you eventually if you aren't offering them what they want, desire and need from a man.

The biggest negative for men with these women is they could end up being one of your worst financial investments ever, because when they decide to leave you there are no refunds. Everything you invested into this relationship is gone without any return on your investment. Between this possibility and divorce in my opinion marriage is a complete roll of the dice for a man. Gambling is not the smartest thing to do with hard earned money.

"The Party Girl" versus "The Play Girl"

The other two women can be great friends, but they are inherently terrible at being in a relationship. This will sound awful, but I tend to feel these two women are disposable, because they feel I am to them. They are the epitome of the phrases, one and done...hit and run. They will literally work against themselves and you if you let them.

See this is their dilemma. They can't commit to one person yet that is what they want. They are perpetual relationship hypocrites. They want to be married but can't focus long enough to invest into the relationship in that manner as the previous two women can focus, enough to accomplish a successful relationship. They are the epitome of one step forward and two steps back.

So don't expect to make too much progress with them. Both of these women are extremely shallow, selfish and non-compassionate unless it benefits them. Both are either distracted or confused. Most of this is sub-conscious. Most don't realize how ugly they actually act because they have been taught and programmed to believe what they do is a normal behavioral occurrence.

Some know exactly what they are doing and actually seek out their prey and victims. The first thing you must acknowledge about these women is you will not ever be the only guy, so if you are emotionally masochistic dive in head first. That was just humor, you must have thick skin and a great deal of tolerance to deal with either of these ladies. The good news if you are the type that likes these types of women is they love a man with stability. They will cling to him and literally drive him crazy if they are given the window of opportunity. They tend to attempt to make and create their ideal man by getting one or two specific characteristics out of several men. They literally see these conquests for different reasons.

They both will have a tendency to cause you to believe they are a different person. They will literally send a representative personality out to meet you until they decide that you can join their club or you can't join and then the real personality will appear. Or should I say one of them because they usually have two. One is negative and hurtful and the other will be nice when she needs you. They both love to be spoiled.

They both literally live up to the nick names I gave them. They want to be entertained. They want to laugh. They can't stand emotional pressure, so don't try to pressure them into a relationship. They will replace you with another guy. So decide who you want to be with them before you get those goo goo eyes for them and never let them steer you away from those goals with them. Never develop intimate feelings for either of them. They will attempt to put you in a category and keep you there.

Once they decide where they want you, it is difficult without a certain skill set to maneuver yourself to the position you want to play. It's best to stay aloof with them until you know what you want from them and what you are willing to give up for them. You can't come to them as some kind of Prince Charming, riding in on your trusty stallion to sweep them off their feet. If that's what you had in mind, run away and don't look back.

They will see you coming a mile away and have a trap set for you when you arrive. Oh and they work well on the fly, so the element of surprise may not always work either.

The Party Girl is really not going to have time for you unless you are spoiling her or she needs you for something. The term using you should come to mind. The Party Girls has so many distractions, from what to wear, who to go with, what club to go too and so many other trivial things that occupy their thoughts. They don't take your life seriously, so don't get offended when they play you to the left or take you for granted......expect it. Chances are there are other guys they care about more than you. You may also be a sixth man or back up, so keep that in mind.

The differences between the Party Girl and the Play girl are very similar to the differences of the Daddy's Girl and the Church Girl, however The Play Girl is confused, so keep this in mind. Although all four have similar personality characteristics, she has a different dynamic than the other three.

The Play Girl may not let you know her dirty thoughts as a Party Girl and Daddy's Girl will, unless she wants to throw you a curve ball which she will often. She may not go to church frequently but still may have the mentality of one that does. She will let you try to seduce her often and seemingly never give in, when the Party Girls might give in if no other guy occupies the sex relationship for her.

Party Girls will talk about the dirty things in her mind like the Daddy's Girl, but doesn't want you focused on them all the time. The Play Girl is unstable and will constantly throw you mixed signals because she is confused as I said earlier. The Play Girl has no idea what she wants, but she does know what she doesn't want.

The Party Girl can kick it with any man except a man with her personality. This man scares the hell out of her. The Party Girl tends to need emotional worship whereas the Play Girl is nervous and paranoid. They will both leave you eventually if they feel that the excitement is gone from them dating you or you don't spoil them enough. Now to keep all this in the same subject matter as this manuscript, you will pay for the whole journey with all four of these women, whether you stay together or not.

So this can be a gamble or an investment. So ask yourself this before your pupils dilate over someone; can you afford the relationship with them and maintain the life plans and the quality of life you've accomplished and are working towards?

CHAPTER 12

THE COVER CHARGE

Alcohol is a social drug that tends to be very addictive. It can come in the form of beer, wine and liquor. It can be positive or negative to a person, depending on how much they consume on a regular basis. It is almost always a staple refreshment at any general social gathering. It is the topic of major advertising campaigns, whether the prevention of abuse, wisdom about the amount of consumption and of course the fun of pounding a few back.

Alcohol has been in existence for centuries. As the saying goes, one must drink responsibly or abstinence is always best. It can be extremely negative or it can have positive side effects. When alcohol is abused, it becomes a psychiatric problem. Alcohol abuse is the habitual consumption of large amounts of alcohol even though it causes the consumer negative circumstances. Alcohol abuse is sometimes described as alcoholism.

There are three types of alcoholics: People who are anti-social. People, who have pleasure-seeking tendencies and the last of the three, are those who are anxiety-ridden. The later can go without any alcohol consumption for long periods of time, but will lose control once they do drink some.

Alcohol abuse can cause problems in one's personal relationships, at work, at school and with one's friends. Alcohol abuse can cause serious health problems; such as brain damage, acute liver disease and failure, skin problems, memory loss, enlargement of male breasts, cancer, malnutrition, cardiovascular disease, chronic pancreatitis, erectile dysfunction and can cause damage to the central nervous system.

Alcohol abuse causes many deaths worldwide for a number of reasons. The Centers for Disease Control and Prevention in this country reported that from 2001-2005, there were approximately 79,000 deaths annually blamed on alcohol abuse. DWI (Driving while intoxicated), or DUI (driving under the influence), are acronyms that describe the crime one commits if they operate a motor vehicle while intoxicated with alcohol.

I have seen billboards saying one of these charges could cost one up to $20,000.00, counting court costs, fines, legal fees and missed time from work. It can really add up. So that last shot or drink when you are driving is never worth the risk. One could possibly hurt or kill somebody in an alcohol induced accident. Any of these infractions could land one in jail. I don't know about you, but I am allergic to bars and not the kind you drink in.

There are a few positive benefits from drinking alcohol; however they only exist with moderate consumption. It can be helpful in increasing brain function and helps one be more creative. Red wine is often credited with increasing "good," HDL cholesterol levels. HDL helps clean the body by removing LDL, or "bad," cholesterol. Red Wine can also help to strengthen hearts. Resveratrol might be the ingredient in red wine that helps prevent damage to the blood vessels and reduces low-density lipoprotein (LDL) cholesterol, as well as helps to prevent blood clots. Gargling some whiskey, combined with a spoonful of warm water, can be used to help ease pain by numbing the muscle tissue of a sore throat. I have been told that brandy and whiskey can help ease the symptoms of a cold or the flu. Alcohol can also lower the risk of cardiovascular disease. Again all of these benefits can only come through moderate consumption of alcoholic beverages. Abuse could and most likely will have opposite and extreme adverse effects on human health.

Night Clubs - A nightclub is an entertainment establishment which is usually open for business from the early evening hours until in some cases dawn. Even though it is a place to consume alcohol, a nightclub is different from the regular bar, pub or tavern, because nightclubs usually always have a dance floor and a DJ booth. The music in nightclubs is usually either a live band or, more commonly, a mix of records spun by a DJ. Most clubs or club nights cater to certain music genres, different groups, nationalities and races and or sub cultures.

A nightclub can be something to do to pass the long hours of being alone on the road. Where ever alcohol is being consumed, constant use of wisdom is essential to balance the amount of alcohol consumed. The biggest negative possibility with patronizing any alcohol based establishment is public intoxication and or drunk driving.

One I want to focus on is the financial expense potential. The one thing I can never get a grip on is why is it important to drink top shelf liquor? Top shelf cost more, but has the same negative effects on you as maybe its "well drink" equivalent. People say, so they won't get a hangover. I say drink more water, to this argument. They say because they drink what they can afford. I say a fool and his money are soon parted. They say, they look good with that bottle in the club, take my picture. I say one is born every day. Even though there are even organic vodkas, from my experience there is no way to truly party healthy. Maybe mix it with a high PH water, but the taste would turn most social drinkers off.

Hey, let's make it rain....syke. While I am on this roll, Night Clubs are a good place to meet a party girl or a play girl. They are usually the type of female that must go to the club every weekend, habitually. They don't mind dancing with you for a drink. Most of these females do what I call supplement their entertainment budget by leading men on in order for the men to cover their entertainment expenses that evening. Don't be a trick. Test them by asking them to buy the next round. Watch their facial expression. If this girl gets mad, frowns up or becomes condescending, run. I may have saved you a divorce bill later in life. You can thank me later.

Night Clubs can be a fun experience, but one must always exercise wisdom when dealing with the combination of women and alcohol. That combination can have a really negative effect on the shopper's wallet. Spend wisely and just because one lady is the finest one in the club, doesn't mean you need to waste your money on her. Chances are several men already have that night before you.

Strip Clubs - First off I can't be a hypocrite, strip clubs can be a lot of enjoyment. No question. I love the feeling of a woman rubbing her body up against mine, arousing my groin to a full erection, however self-control is the word. As they say, business before pleasure, your money or bank account is the foundation of your business. Tupac would scream M.O.B. in the street, in the club or on record. Because your business or money in this case is far more important than what that woman is doing for you in the strip club. So leave your wallet in the car and just bring in the amount of money that you can afford to spend and leave any other money at your house. Credit cards, debit cards and check books too. Leave them at home. The club will ask you for I.D. so bring your I.D. with you. There are 8 types of strippers and that's another book. Dare me to write it. Basically you must put some thought and wisdom into every trip to a strip club, because there is always a woman that can and will make you spend your house payment or rent money, so to speak. Keep this in mind. No stripper will stick and stay near you if she believes your loot is low, whether you tell her this or she sees it in your actions. So use that wisdom to get her away from you when you need to push her off. And when that Super Stripper I spoke about earlier shows up, they can only do so much damage. Why, because you thought and planned your spending before you left the house. Because when you are broke you are broke. And for the record when can you afford to blow money? Blowing money is never a good idea unless it helps your health, stimulates your mind or strengthens you physically or spiritually. Keep that in mind. A strip club can improve one's confidence and it is a pleasant distraction, so control yourself and have fun.

Obesity... Who am I to tell someone how to eat? I will keep it real with you however. Some foods have fat in them that clog arteries, which can lead to heart and artery diseases and possibly stroke. Some foods make it very hard on your heart to function properly. Some foods contain chemicals and substances that can cause cancer. Some foods because of their manmade ingredients cause erectile dysfunction. Some foods can cause diabetes. Several leading Cardiologist have gone on record saying a plant based diet is the only way to significantly lower your chances of contracting some of the diseases or ailments I mentioned. Let's keep it real. Cancer was cured in the 1930's by a German doctor named Max Gerson. Unfortunately in this country it is considered holistic. Some people take this farther and become Vegans and Vegetarians. If this is something you may have in mind, just remember any food that had a Mother or had a face is what you should avoid.

Gambling is considered an actual disease. I don't feel it is a disease. Its ones non-ability to say no to ones urges. Lack of self-control is not a disease. It is a mental weakness. Excess is the key word. Anything one finds enjoyable, that he or she may or does have trouble controlling is a potential addiction. Anything done to excess is bad or bad for you. One must live their life in control. Not out of control. Gambling can be addictive. It leaves the person that can't say no to negative urges as helpless as a drug addict. They can potentially lose everything they have worked for all their lives and they can and will lose their dignity and self-respect. The lure of easy money is always enticing. Some people consider gambling entertainment. I personally feel there are a hell of a lot more sensible and responsible things to do for entertainment. One may argue a strip club is in this category because it is also addictive and one just literally gives their money away. The one argument I can give on the strip club side is a man will leave the club with a short boost of confidence which can help him. If you win at gambling you could get a feeling of accomplishment. The big question is if you win. Casinos are in business to make and take money, not to lose it. They are in business to seduce you out of yours. Ever notice how upset they get with people that win well against them. I am sure you have seen TV shows and Movies about Casino owners getting very upset and possibly even becoming violent when someone is winning. They design their systems to not lose, to literally take the money out of your pocket and bank account. When someone is beating them, that someone is a challenge to the Casino's system, income and as with any man, he will protect his lively hood. So how successful should one want to become at this form of "entertainment". I remember visiting Atlantic City and walking into I believe Trump Casino. As I walked slowly through the aisles I noticed people playing slots. These people had expressionless faces. Like Zombies. Some glossy eyes like a crack head that just got a hit recently. Almost robotically, they pull the lever with one hand and stuff coins in the machine, one at a time with the other and somehow managing to drink alcohol or coffee at the same time. A few years ago and old acquaintance of mine talked me into going to one of Windsor Ontario's casinos. I was on a contract, so money was pretty good for me. This acquaintance was unemployed. I was single with a 12 year old and he was married with two children and one infant. I decided I could blow $35.00, so that's all I put in my pocket when we left. Together he and his wife both had about $180.00 to their name. He took all of it. When we got to the casino he saw a very attractive black jack dealer and sat down at her table and started flirting. I walked over to the slot machines and started blowing my money. About 15 minutes later, I had blown the entire $35.00. I walked back over to the table he was playing black jack at to tell him I was ready to go back to Detroit. I sat down nearby and watched. This guy was smiling more pleasantly than I had ever seen him prior. The dealer was very serious and would only briefly grin at times. She took all of his money and he was still smiling. I don't have an explanation for these stories; I just thought these memories had relevance to this subject matter. Anytime something in life takes control of you and you lose control of your proper decision making, then one needs to clean house. People clean house a number of ways from Church, to mental therapy, meditation, prayer or some people just stop. Some people say it is a form of entertainment and I imagine if watching your hard earned money leave you is fun for you then it is entertainment for you.

CHAPTER 13

MAN MADE DRUGS

This world is such a negative place. To think people actually sit back and think of ways to cause people turmoil in their life. Man Made drugs are the product of such negative thoughts.

Prescription drugs, their side effects and the drug chain reaction..... They've got a drug for the original drug's side effect, and a drug for the side effect that the next drug caused and a drug for the next drug's side effect and so on and so on. Most prescription drugs have many side effects. Up to and including death.

Do the Math. Dayum! Now where I come from, that ain't just a hook up, but that is a hustle. Naw...... that's big time hustling. Foe Show. As an engineer and product designer, I have a moral obligation to produce product lines that work. I am not allowed to put out flawed product. When the auto makers put out a vehicle with a flaw, there is a recall. Flawed products can and will potentially cause injury or harm to the public and Yo Gubna won't allow us in the manufacturing industry to produce inferior products. However the drug companies can and do put out flawed product and it's completely legal.

Synthetic and toxic narcotics are pushed on us every day by Yo Gubna and their potna, capitalistic big business. I can hear one of their TV commercials now. This wonderful delightful music. Funny, I can always hear that word death in the side effects loud and clear. Let me get this straight.....you want me to use a drug I could possibly over dose and die on? Seriously?

Doctor's, wanted me to take Beta Blockers for my blood pressure and congestive heart failure caused by my previous diet and cigars. I was such a meat eater. They should call that bullshit Alpha blockers, because it literally turns men into women. Why? It causes erectile dysfunction. No worries though, they have a drug called Viagra to help you out.

What pissed me off is Calcium Channel Blockers help the cardio vascular system in the same manner as Alpha Blockers. Oh Sorry. Beta Blockers, however do not cause penis problems. Interesting.......Viagra or sildenafil citrate can cause the penis to become erect or hard again while taking Beta Blockers. However if you have an erection that lasts more than 4 hours, they have a penis injection waiting for you. . Ask Chris Rock. If it is not treated right away, a man can have permanent penis damage. However for me Viagra didn't work, however an Alkaline or high PH diet did for me.

Let's play a game. I will name the Viagra side effect and you name the next drug in the chain reaction to treat that side effect. Sudden vision loss in one or both eyes can be a condition called non-arteritic anterior ischemic optic neuropathy. The possibility of sudden decrease in hearing or a complete hearing loss. Okay I know those are hard, but here are some easy ones. There have been complaints of—

- Ringing in the ears or dizziness
- Headache
- Flushin
- Upset stomach
- Abnormal vision, such as changes in color vision like a blue color tinge and blurred vision. (Dayum, that sounds like an acid trip to me.)
- Stuffy or runny nose
- Back pain
- Muscle pain
- Nausea and rashes.

Viagra also has more side effects, but you should consult your doctor to learn more. Now... Check it out. That's some big time hustlin.

Methamphetamine, otherwise known as meth, crystal, chalk, and ice is a stimulant. It is classified as a Schedule II drug, which means, one can only get some with a prescription that cannot be refilled. It has chemical characteristics similar to an amphetamine. It is usually white, is a bitter-tasting powder and has no smell. User's usually smoke or snort it. They also dissolve it up in a liquid and shoot it up in a syringe.

Smoking or injecting methamphetamine, gets it to the brain very quickly. Long-term methamphetamine use causes weight loss, bad teeth and poor oral health, and skin sores caused by intense scratching. As with several other man made drugs the high is very intense, but usually doesn't last very long. This causes a user to smoke or use more, just trying to stay high.

Dopamine is what causes us to feel motivation and pleasure. Methamphetamine will increase the amount of dopamine the body produces. Methamphetamine releases dopamine in certain pleasure areas of the brain and because of this it is a very addictive substance. People who use methamphetamine for long periods of time usually experience anxiety, confusion, insomnia, mood swings and often can have a very violent behavior and personality. They may act paranoid, and complain of seeing and hearing things.

Chronic methamphetamine usage will also cause chemical and molecular damage to the brain. Imaging studies have shown that methamphetamine has a lot to do with reduced motor skills and impaired verbal learning. Studies have shown that habitual meth users may experience severe structural and functional problems in areas of the brain that control emotion and memory. Some of these negative brain issues continue after one quits using methamphetamine.

Heroin, aka boy, or dem blues, H, smack, horse, brown, black, tar are just a few of the slang names given this opiate over the years. Heroin was invented by Charles Romley Alder Wright in the year 1874. He added two acetyl groups to the molecule morphine. It is in the opium poppy. This is a very nasty drug. Heroin has very dangerous effects. It can weaken the body's ability to create dopamine. It is usually taken by smoking, snorting, or shooting it up in a syringe.

Injecting heroin is the most life threatening because it is often cut with other substances to increase profits. When not mixed properly, blood vessels that lead to the heart, kidneys and brain can become clogged. And as everyone knows AIDS or hepatitis can be caught if a needle has been shared that was previously used by someone infected with the diseases. Heroin causes what is called withdrawal:

Known symptoms of this are—

- Diarrhea
- Nausea
- Vomiting
- Insomnia
- Muscle and bone pain
- Panic attacks and loss of appetite
- Nose bleeds and convulsions

Being a creative type myself, I cherish other creative people. I enjoy their expressions communicated through their art form. Heroin has taken so many wonderful and talented people from us.

- Janis Joplin was an extremely popular legendary singer and songwriter in the late sixties. She struggled with heroin addiction throughout her career. She died at the age of 27 from a heroin overdose
- Guitarist and song writer Jimi Hendrix used many different types of drugs, including LSD, heroin, and amphetamines. He died in 1970 of a drug overdose.
- River Phoenix, who acted in films such as Indiana Jones and the Last Crusade and Stand by Me, died in 1993 from a reported heroin overdose.
- American graffiti artist Jean-Michel Basquiat died at the age of twenty-seven of a heroin overdose. He garnered critical acclaim when he rose to stardom in the 1980s.

- Comedic actor Chris Farley struggled with addiction to various drugs, including heroin, for many years. He was discovered dead in his apartment in October, 1997. Farley was 33 years old.
- Standup comedian Lenny Bruce was a very controversial comedic artist. He was known for his drug abuse and using profanity on stage. He reportedly overdosed on heroin and died in 1966.

Powder Cocaine, girl, snow. Or how about crack, hard, work or does Free Base sound more familiar. All are descriptions of variations of creations made from the coca plant.

Being a male of African descent, I could find this next fact quite humorous. Well if I could look at it from a non-empathetic point of view, but since that is impossible I am terribly insulted that the law is not publicly rewritten.

Cocaine and other opiates were legal at one time. Sears Roebuck used to sell cocaine already in the syringe ready for you to shoot up. Cocaine as well as other substances thought of as drugs at the time such as marijuana were made illegal and criminalized because of racial insecurities of law makers at the turn of the century. The law maker's at the time played on fears of so called "drug crazed negroes" and made references to black men under the influence of drugs, murdering whites in some kind of justified revengeful moment for the extreme cruelty of slavery.

Dr. Hamilton Wright, testified at a hearing for the Harrison Act about this subject. Wright alleged that drugs made blacks uncontrollable and gave them superhuman powers and caused them to rebel against white authority. Dr. Christopher Koch of the State Pharmacy Board of Pennsylvania testified that "Most of the attacks upon the white women of the South are the direct result of a cocaine-crazed Negro brain". On February 8, 1914, The New York Times published an article called "Negro Cocaine 'Fiends' Are New Southern Menace: Murder and Insanity Increasing Among Lower-Class Blacks" by Edward Huntington Williams, reported that Southern sheriffs increased the caliber of their guns and ammo from .32 to .38 to make sure these Negroes under the effect of cocaine died when shot.

Despite the extreme racialization of the issue that took place in the build up to the Act's passage, most research on this subject showed that black Americans were using cocaine and opium much less than white Americans. Crack cocaine was introduced into the Black urban areas of most of the U.S. cities in my opinion to de-stabilize the black communities in this country and take their newly established middle class status and their real estate at prices way below market value.

In urban areas across the country once thriving black middle class communities now resemble more of a war zone then a safe middle class neighborhood. The lure of easy money from crack cocaine sales caused an internal sui-genocide amongst black people or the descendants of <u>NON</u>. Black on Black crime is what the media eventually called it.

Gary Indiana was the third largest city in the state of Indiana in the year 1980. It had a population of 161,000 and growing. Due to layoffs at the steel mills, the developing crack industry and gang war fare as a result led to the population dropping to 60,000 today. Most of this population drop was due to murders and flight. Gary was the nation's murder capital for years. In 1997 HHN Records released the record Steel City which brought to light to the eventual demise of this once thriving black middle class city.

Free Base is a way of using cocaine and is extremely dangerous one; using a fire accelerant to have a constant flame to inhale the cocaine at will. Richard Pryor, the greatest comedic mind ever in my opinion was a free base addict. One of the unfortunate things he is remembered for is his infamous fire run, on a free base induced high. Funny thing....This temporarily drug crazed negro, only hurt himself and sure as hell didn't gain super human strength either.

Bath Salt - Bath salts can be snorted, smoked, injected or swallowed. Bath salts users have claimed to experience symptoms like headaches, irregular heartbeat, nausea, hallucinations, paranoia, dehydration, panic attacks and the deterioration of skeletal muscle tissue. The News Media has reported that the use of this substance could cause one to become violent. Other health problems include kidney failure, liver failure and one could possibly develop suicidal tendencies.

Tobacco Products - Cigarettes, cigars, pipe tobacco and chewing tobacco are manufactured using the leaves of the tobacco plant. They are processed to be extremely addictive. Quite a few chemicals are added to the leaf so they can burn longer periods of time when smoking. There are more than 4,000 potentially harmful chemicals added to this product. Of these, more than 50 are said to be carcinogenic, which can cause several types of cancer. Some of these chemicals are:

- Benzene - which is a colorless hydrocarbon made from petroleum and coal. It is used in the chemical manufacturing industry and as a petrol additive.
- Ammonia helps the conversion of nicotine to gas. It is used as a flavoring and the main ingredient in dry cleaning solvents as well as toilet cleaners.
- Formaldehyde is highly poisonous and is used as a preservative for dead people. It is a colorless liquid and extremely carcinogenic in nature.
- Tar is also contained in tobacco products. More than 70% of the tar gets trapped in the lungs of smokers.
- Hydrogen cyanide is a salt of hydrocyanic acid. It is the same substance that is present in gas chamber poison used in executions.
- Carbon monoxide - the gas that is found in the exhaust of cars.
- Arsenic is a powdered trioxide used in manufacturing glass and also as a pesticide and rat poison.
- Tobacco products are said to contain rat poison as well. Rat poisons contain arsenic. There are many types of rat poison ingredients contained in cigarettes. Rat poisons contain arsenic, and several coagulants like brodifacoum, warfarin, diphacinone, and bromadiolon, metal phosphides, and a large amount of vitamin D. It is suggested that sodium fluoride, oxalic acid, barium carbonate, and several such chemicals are also present in rat poison. There is a significant amount of fluorine present in cigarettes (rat poison contains sodium fluoride). It was admitted during court testimony that coumarin was used for adulteration in cigarettes.

Some other popular drugs that are used recreationally are; Ecstasy, LSD, PCP, Angel Dust, Adderall, Xanax, Benzodiazepines and Vicodin.

Why is it that regular people are incarcerated for years or life and sometimes executed when they put these types of ingredients in people's foods and drinks?

Why are tobacco manufacturers held harmless for making their products potentially deadly over time by using all these poisons?

Both intentionally and knowingly put the chemicals in the consumable, knowing the damage it will cause a fellow human being. I am just curious. A doctor once asked me why did I feel the need to smoke when I did. I told her I had no idea and she should ask Phillip Morris. She didn't find that humorous. I did.

A former girlfiend of mine smoked and drank heavily for years among other things. I first witnessed her smoking as a teenager when we were in high school. I was always unsuccessful at trying to motivate her to get some control over the habits. I believe that was because she lived such a hard life and she was too damaged emotionally to muster the strength to attempt to control the habit. Cigarettes ravaged her body and she succumbed very quickly to lung cancer and died.

Recreational, my ass. These negative devices will destroy your moral core. Some of this shit will make you rob your Mother, prostitute your body, end up in the penitentiary for using or even dealing, because using is expensive.

Manmade drugs will cause you all sorts of mental, physical, financial, family and spiritual problems that no one needs in their life. Period. Don't let these evil and very negative traps destroy you and your life. If you see this crap on your journey....keep it moving, for your sake. Hopefully this chapter on manmade drugs will help you stay on your course to your goals and dreams.

CHAPTER 14

ENSURING YOUR SUCCESS.

Over the past 25 years I have seen a lot of changes in the contract engineering world. I have had to reinvent myself at times just to stay relevant. I have taught myself new software and industries on the fly just to stay competitive. I've been modifying my resume as well, in this case cutting off all those eighties jobs, so I appear younger. What makes absolutely no sense to me is the way corporations think and go about screening new employees.

They don't necessarily want the best person for the job. It still amazes me that someone fresh out of college can get a job before me and they in some cases have no viable work experience. Corporations want degrees, not proven skilled professionals for the most part. They would rather struggle and look good on paper than actually put the best person in that position. When I start my electronics company, I plan to hire the best people for the job. I don't care if they have a degree or not. My question is, can they do the job effectively? If that answer is yes, do they have a personality that is easy to inter act with? If both of these answers are yes, that is my candidate for my empty position. I don't care if they are a member of the club or not.

The old school job shoppers had a code that everyone tried to follow. The new school job shopper is self-centered, somewhat arrogant at times and has no respect for the old heads. When I started job shopping, shopper's looked out for each other, even if they had nothing in common. It was indeed a code of ethics. We'd be our own loan institutions. We were very generous with the town knowledge, as far as places to eat, motel prices, drinks and partying. Usually there was at least one shopper that had information the new guy needs. Now, all that attitude and empathy for each other is gone. Everyone looks out for themselves.

One thing my Mother always told me and it still rings true today is to avoid all religious, personalisms and political conversations. These conversations almost always end in an argument, especially if the parties involved are from different religions or cultures. When you think about religion, think about it this way. All religion that has a one God philosophy, all originated from one Middle Eastern doctrine.

That doctrine basically divided into three sections. This was the first major separation. Judaism, Christianity and Islam were formed from this division, with Islam and Judaism both worshiping God directly, while Christians, worship Jesus as well. These three base religions exist because people were arguing way back in history.

Think about it, if the arguments or disagreements were solved there wouldn't be three base religions. There would be two or even one again. So these conversations to this day are disagreements waiting to happen.

There is no place for negativity in the work place or anywhere for that fact. Everyone feels their -ism is the best and usually are prepared to defend it to the death in some cases. Also avoid showing any political opinions or affiliations. As with religions, everyone feels their party is best. The one thing I noticed about politics is people get offended if you don't think like they do. I am what I guess you would call an independent. So I couldn't win in a room full of democrats, libertarians or republicans.

People take political issues seriously. Historically people have sacrificed their lives for political opinions. People have been killed for having political opinions. Even light harmless conversations can be remembered by people and get you pulled into uncomfortable situations and conversations that you normally avoid later like one of these three.

In every walk of life there is a chain of command. The work place is no different. One must do their best to never go over a supervisors head. Sometimes you have to do what you have to do, but a general rule of thumb is to always respect and honor the chain of command. Never outshine your supervisor or anyone above your pay grade. Sometimes it is better to just be humble and let your supervisor shine. You are there for a pay check, not to win a popularity contest. Try to not be a yes man or a no man. Just be honorable and dependable. Never say what you can do if you have doubts without taking the time to think about it with some wisdom. Always guess two and a half times what you think it will take to do a job.

Humility is always the best approach to success. No one likes or appreciates the cocky or over confident individual. Confidence, not over confidence garners respect. Humility and warm moods invite people to have positive feelings about you.

The combination of the two, in the right amounts, will keep one in good standing with supervisors and co-workers. This professional attitude along with a diligent work effort will put one in the position to always be considered for advancement under the ideal circumstances. So whether your circumstances are good or not, you need to have the best attitude possible no matter what the circumstances are until you can put yourself in a better position.

It is said that humility is not thinking less of yourself, but it is really thinking of yourself less. They say pride can change an angel into a devil. They also say humility can turn a man into an angel. Pride can make you fake, but humility makes you real. With pride comes so many curses, meanwhile humility brings you great blessings.

Never break any laws, company compliances or your own moral rules. A company's procedures are guide lines to lead employees into making logical decisions to achieve sound and rational outcomes. Rules and laws are in place to keep things a certain way. In a company atmosphere, policies and rules are there to enable the company to be at its best level of product production and efficiency. .

Everything has a price. There is no free lunch. As the saying goes, if it is too good to be true, then it probably is. Beware the great deal, dust your spider senses off.

I am not saying if someone has a great deal for you to consider it a scam. I am saying take the time to investigate it properly. Ask questions in order to ascertain what is really going on in the deal. Examine both sides. Ask yourself why the person is offering such a deal. Empathize with them to see if you can see a scam in the works. No man wants to be someone's mark.

Everything has a window for the best success. Patience and wisdom need to be applied when looking for the right moments to act on your intentions and goals. Patience is the ability to accept or tolerate delay, trouble, or suffering without getting angry or upset. To be patient one must be the master of his or her emotions. One must not attempt to go thru the window too early or too late. One must be constantly aware and paying attention so their timing is perfect. One may not get a second chance, so accuracy is essential to your success factor.

One needs to always pay attention to detail and be willing to do more than expected. Being willing to go the extra mile for a supervisor or loved one is a key indicator of how engaged a person is. If they feel valued and not taken for granted, they feel a sense of loyalty to their supervisor or loved one. People are much more likely to do more than expected when it's necessary.

The motivation for employees to do that can often come from their level of job satisfaction. If they feel inspired and believe they can make a meaningful and valued contribution to the product goal. Having a workforce that wants to do more than expected will have positive benefits for employers and corporations, This ensures a notably higher level of productivity, less employee turnover and reduced amount of sick days taken.

Be slow to speak and quick to listen. The bible says this and even an atheist that has wisdom would say it is true. I have never been very good at arguing or winning debates. So this tactic is always best for someone like me. Also it's a good way to learn things about someone if you can listen objectively. I tell people all the time that the quickest way to get to know someone is to shut up and listen. A person will answer all questions if you ask the right questions and listen for the right answers.

Trying to out-talk someone is never a good idea. Some feel this is the only way to communicate, as if it is some kind of verbal competition. Be patient. Pay attention to the speaker and resign that some of your comments don't really need to be mentioned. If mentioning them will lead you into a heated debate or argument, I would say just listen. Some people feel everything is an argument. Arguments rarely solve any problems, however cool, calm conversations can work every time.

Procrastination vs. Persistence - Procrastination can destroy any effort and all dreams while persistence can give one anything they desire. Some people never get anything done, because they constantly put things off till tomorrow. A person that is persistent embraces the challenge whether they like it or not and hang in there until the task is complete. Procrastination is putting off or delaying a task or problem, especially something requiring immediate attention. While persistence is the quality that allows someone to continue doing something or trying to do something even though it is difficult or opposed by other people.

CHAPTER 15

DEFENSIVE STRATEGIES.

We all must do our best to ignore negative influences. Out of sight can mean, out of mind. And out of mind is what we are striving for. As I mentioned earlier the mind can only be negative or positive. Even when we are not mentally conscious of negative input entering our minds, it will. This is why it is so important to constantly program our own subconscious minds so that it will work like a white blood cell fighting enemies of the body, it should attack negative input and force it from the mind, before it can spread and engulf one's thought patterns.

The thing I have learned about negative energy is it can kill, steal and destroy everything you are. A negative mind will compound the devastating effects of diseases. Negative thoughts and actions can destroy a life or career. Negative thoughts can destroy you via depression and suicide. Stay away from miserable people. These people are a cancer on the mind of a positive person. So as you know in this country there are only two legal ways to fight cancer and that's radiation (can't use that one it's murder) and a biopsy. Cut the person off and out of your life. Even if they seem to change, this is still no reason to let your guard down. A person will always return to their true self, so just be patient and wait for that to happen. That way you determine if it is all an act or not. Don't confuse sadness or depression with misery. Even positive people have bad periods. Again wait and see who they really are. Be a fly on the wall.

Protect your reputation. Negative people love throwing dirt at positive people and for no logical reason. Negative people usually are tight with a few negative emotions and horde these emotions like that new man toy or a lady and her favorite pair of shoes. A good reputation is needed to advance in life towards ones goals and dreams or make successful accomplishments. Protect your life and reputation as if it is your only one, which is the case in reality. Never let anyone negative close to you or the people in your inner circle.

People change sides and alliances all the time. Never trust anyone professionally. I have had a couple so-called fiancé's tell me negative about someone they know. Get me to feel the same way as them about those people or some of their deeds and they would change sides and leave me looking like the villain, when they had seduced me down that negative path. So if a couple of my so-called fiancé's would pull off betrayal like this what will a co-worker do to you?

Misery loves company; no one wants to be miserable alone. They need to share their negativity with someone. The negative emotions are as infectious as a communicable disease. Someone else's negativity can take your life, take your money, take your wife and or your children. The avoidance of negative people is a life task that will never be completed or fully accomplished. You are engaged in a never ending journey to bliss. Your avoidance of people that use negative emotions needs to be a labor of love.

Always come across as a Friend even when dealing with your enemy; this will always keep your enemy off balance and unsure what to expect from you. Study your rivals, opponents and enemies. Keep them in your thoughts. Watch how they deal with their known enemies and adversaries and remember how they responded to attacks. Always pay attention to what is being said about your enemies. Send other's to find out the validity of the gossip.

Do not offend anybody; Always make a habit of not offending people. Causing negative emotions has no benefits to you at all, unless you need a person to lose control of their thinking. This can and will create a new enemy

Never take sides. Always stay neutral. It is unwise to rush to take sides. Your only loyalty should be to you and your inner circle and only as long as they deserve it. By maintaining your independence, you have room to maneuver, plot, plan and calibrate. Only commit to yourself. Neutrality gives you the room and flexibility to move and survive.

Go to bed every night knowing you did no man foul or negatively; this way you won't have to look over your shoulder about something you did in the past that might cause one to seek revenge against you.

Beware the deal too good to be true; nothing comes for free, unless its source is from within your inner circle. The only good deal I would trust is from someone I trust. The problem is you can only fully trust yourself and because you are human, you have to take yourself with a grain of salt as well. Any deal too good to be true, needs to be thoroughly investigated. One should pay attention to the body language, facial expressions and statements of the one selling the deal before and after hearing the sales pitch. This is too be able to determine how inaccurate the seller maybe or how dishonest they are.

Never allow greed to take control of you; greed is a very intense and selfish desire for wealth, power, food or any highly valued commodity. Greed fueled the British Empire and was passed down to its offspring the U.S.A. Greed fueled the Nazi's. Greed fueled Manifest Destiny. Greed fueled the south and convinced them to use slave labor to increase their profits. The use of greed can and has started wars. Caused millions to suffer and die. Greed gave some individuals God complexes, like the audacity to rob someone of their God given culture and attempt to replace it with a foreign one. "We will make good Englishmen out of these savages". The Bible or the Gun was the choice given to the conquered. Accept Jesus Christ as your Lord and Savior or die!

I often wonder if these individuals were shown a mirror and put them through the same evil negativity would it cure them of the evil that was dwelling inside of them. Greed is an obsession. No obsession is good, because it reorders your priorities. Greed can be your Achilles Heel.

Everybody has a weakness or an Achilles heel. Find your enemies weakness and attack it relentlessly. The leader is always the weakest link in any group. Always crush your enemy totally and completely. Never stop halfway. The enemy can get a second life or breath and come back to attack you again, maybe with an advantage over you. As in the David and Goliath story, Goliath was feared for being a giant and a fierce warrior. By slaying the giant David gained famed fortune and became a King. He didn't stop halfway. He didn't show the giant any mercy. He slew the giant. Common sense told David, he better kill Goliath, because Goliath would surely kill him easily if he was to survive the wrath of David.

In most wars or battles each side makes a strategic effort to bring down the leader of the opposing army. As with anything severing, the mind from the body causes chaos. As a child my cousin and I were in my aunt's back yard with her and a friend of hers. She had bought a live chicken. She asked her friend to behead the chicken for her. When the chickens head was cut off it ran around the yard in a panic. This is what will most likely happen to any army, gang or group that is completely mentally dependent on its leader. They will lose their ability to think rationally as a group as previously under the command of their leader and start thinking irrationally.

Act like it's your last chance to succeed. All people are at their best when they really want something and in their mind they believe it's the last chance they are going to get. You must feel a sense of urgency.

Discover people's weaknesses in case they become an enemy. Emotional ones as well as professional. You will need both if you get in a battle. No positive person wants to fight someone verbally or physically. Negative people will try you so you need to be able to do them in as quickly as possible and using the least amount of energy doing it. They are not worth the energy needed or used for the breath to say their names.

Avoid telling anyone that doesn't have a need to know your personal business at work. People have a tendency to get your information and consider it public domain. Your personal business can become a water cooler or coffee break room topic of conversation. No one wants to walk in on people saying negative things about them and laughing. This is another reason why you can't care what people think about you. What they say can affect you negatively so one must not feed the negative energy here, by discussing one's personal business at work. People may call you anti-social…let them. Who cares? Your private business is private for a reason.

Any human being in life, as well as in the work environment that ever displays multiple personalities, mood swings or emotions must be avoided if they can't be eliminated from your life. These people have issues that may not be diagnosable without a psychology degree. The problem with this person is they are emotionally volatile and could have an outburst that affects you negatively. They are usually very emotionally excitable, so one must keep them calm if you are forced to be around them.

Keep your ambitions in your mind only. They can drum up jealousy and envy from your enemies. Never think out loud. Speak as little as possible and still get your point across. Keep your ambitions in your mind only. Your plans, goals and dreams can drum up jealousy and envy from your enemies, family members and co-workers. A strategy I have problems with at times is thinking out loud. Don't ever do this; if you can help it.

Don Corleone, the patriarch of the fictional **Godfather** movies, made a statement that sticks with me like glue. That statement was never let anyone know what you are thinking. Now a job shopper's life has no comparison to a mafia style life, however, whenever money is involved the less people know about your plans is always better. Your mention of your plans may let someone know you want the same thing that they do. Now you have competition or a possible enemy. Speak as little as possible and still get your point across is a rule of thumb in this case.

Elaboration can be your worst enemy. Elaboration is a form of babbling. Babbling is annoying to listen to. Even though elaboration can be good when spoken with wisdom, intelligence, confidence and factual data, it is always better if it can be said with a minimum amount of words and phrases.

Never argue with anyone. Let your actions argue for you. Actions speak louder than words. Arguing is an angry form of conversation that can get heated. So if arguing is a product of negative emotions then this conversation needs to be neutral if it can't be a positive one. IF an argument cannot be downgraded to a normal conversation, you need to politely excuse yourself. This is a time when maintaining your positive mindset will be difficult.

Pay attention to everyone and everything. One must be aware of everything going on around them. I don't know if you have seen any of the Sherlock Holmes, Robert Downey Jr. movies, but Mr. Holmes is very aware of everything around him. He notices and remembers subtle things like the color of a feather in a person's hat or a red stain on a shirt that has a unique tint to it. CIA agents have to learn this skill when going to work for the government.

Never take anything at work personally. It's only work, it's not your life. Never take your work emotions home after the end of your shift. Never take your personal life to work. Work and your personal life must be kept separate in your mind as much as possible. The less overlap you have the less possibility you have of exposing your personal business at work and alienating someone in your personal life.

"Guilty by association". This is a concept one must be very aware of. Even if you don't do certain things, people will assume you do because of your affiliation with a person. If a person is gay and you are seen frequently with them, a negative mind will make assumptions. If a person is a drug addict or alcoholic or any other title that can be considered negative, a negative mind will imagine and believe you are the same as the person you are with at the moment. So because of these negative assumptions, here are some people you should avoid and beware of at work and in life. I call these individuals professional leaches;

- Ones that bite the hand that feeds them and don't respect the person that is making their life easier.
- Ones that do no work yet demand compensation as if they did work.
- Ones that do work that doesn't help the cause or is a wastes of company's time.
- Ones that have no respect for the cause or effort of the department or company.

These people can give you a bad reputation at work. And as I said previously one must protect their reputation because reputation equals income which equals your quality of life.

CHAPTER 16

OFFENSIVE STRATEGIES.

Use the rule, kill them with kindness. Kindness is a very powerful weapon, because it is very difficult to naturally defend yourself against it. The fact that it has no negative bi-products, it is extremely difficult to counter. It's easier to submit to it than to stand against it. One must really try hard to do this, but then once this happens, you can see them trying. It's difficult to argue, hate or even frown at someone when they smile genuinely at you. Smiling is a great form of defense, as well as a sure fire, guaranteed way of determining who is on your side and who is not, as I mentioned in an earlier chapter.

Be a good team player. Some of my favorite basketball players are point guards. Point guards are the quarterbacks on a conventional basketball team. In today's game, however all of the players at any position have developed their passing skills. Forwards and Centers are getting more assists than guards at times. On today's basketball teams it doesn't matter who gets the assist and who scores as long as the team is working together in an unselfish manner to succeed and win the game.

Let this rule apply to you. However, the work world is not a basketball court and other factors come into play. One must pick and choose with wisdom who to pass too. There are times when you should assist an enemy as well as a friend. One must be careful with this and be able to look beyond the moment and develop a level of intuition about what will happen after your pass. Who will witness the pass? Who will the pass effect. What will the pass effect. If the outcome is consistent with your goals then by all means pass the ball. If you see a cost that is too much to sacrifice or pay then try dribbling a little longer before you make that assist.

Be a part of a productive team by using your wisdom and problem solving skills to help your team succeed.

Always Say Less than Necessary; some people give me the impression they really love to hear themselves speak. They will string sentence after sentence on to sound intelligent on a specific subject. No effective speaker rambles.

Being human beings, we make mistakes. So the less you speak, it makes sense to think that, the less chance you have of making a speaking error. The term quotable comes to mind. A quotable is a statement or phrase that is wise, astounding, hilarious or just very memorable. They are usually short, sweet and to the point. When one elaborates, the meaning is sometimes diluted or loses its punch or impact. When attempting to impress someone, the less you say while still maintaining merit, the more respectable you will seem or appear. People that are respected, get respect by using a quotable or an impact statement.

Attract the people you want and need around you; let's put a recap on Chapter 2 and constantly remind ourselves to remember to search for these types of people.

Remember to only add these types of people into your inner circle. Use the six question test to determine if you should allow this person into your life or possibly make someone your spouse or significant other. Will the two of you share compassion, empathy and respect with each other? Do both of you follow the two way street principle and will you always treat each other with the philosophy of the Golden Rule?

Protect these people from the people that use the negative emotions. Collect them into social media communities, or start clubs with them. Go into business ventures with them. Enjoy common hobbies with them.

Communicate with them openly without damaging the relationship. Teach them to recruit like-minded people as well. There is strength in numbers.

Lead effectively and demand respect by your actions; Actions speak louder than words. One should always lead by example, not by force or threat. When you lead by example you command respect that is voluntarily given. Any respect that has to be created via negative emotions is weak and vulnerable to attack, because of the dissent and chaos it causes in the minds of the people on the receiving end of the negativity.

Maintaining neutrality until the wind blows so to speak is always a good position to be in because one can maneuver oneself into a safe or comfortable position. Showing good behavior and manners are essential to demanding respect. A pleasant personality, whenever possible, helps one gain admiration from those that you lead. Being Empathetic and respectful is always a good way to be towards your subordinates.

A good leader must be willing to work more than anyone else. Learn everyone's job well enough to be empathetic and take the blame and responsibility for any failure that his team encounters. A good leader must be available but not wear out his welcome which erodes the respect that is earned. Arguing is a negative waste of time. It usually offends the other person and can only amplify the negative emotions already being used. If you are around people that you seem to argue with often then they are not people you should constantly be around (if you can help it), until the arguing is controlled or eliminated.

Asking for help…Asking for help is an art form and requires a certain skill set. No one ever wants to feel needy, but at times we all need help. How to ask effectively needs to be done in a way that leaves the potentially helpful person comfortable with having the conversation with you.

Inner circle people are there for a reason. You are in their inner circle for the same reason. When you feel the need to ask for help, never bring up the past. Sometimes those incidents are not completely positive on both sides and if you are not having an empathetic memory you run the risk of them having a bad memory of that moment. If there is a way for the helpful person to benefit from helping you, turn your request in to a non-annoying sales pitch.

Be courteous and appreciative. Be humble and never come across dominant or demanding. The most important aspect or role you must play in this one-sided transaction is to be honest, make sure you keep your word and do precisely as you said you would. In the event you find it impossible to keep your word, communicate with the person immediately and as often as you would want to be contacted about someone owing you money or a favor. Never give them a reason or need to come and ask you any questions about the transaction. Keep everything on the table in plain view, so to speak. That way they stay in your inner circle. If you do this properly you may become closer, because they have seen proof they can trust you.

Re-Invent yourself...Sometimes life has a way of pigeon holing you into a stall or dead end pattern or position. Never accept your current circumstances as a permanent situation. One must constantly improve oneself and always be on the hunt for windows of opportunity. Sometimes if your ideal position or way to earn income doesn't exist, create a way to achieve the goal. Man is only confined to the limits of what he or she believes they can or cannot do. Where there is a will, there is a way. You are traveling several straight lines or paths to your goals and dreams in life. Constantly calibrate to stay on your path.

Always keep your confidence and humility in check. Too much of either one will cause you problems. Displaying too much confidence can be construed to be arrogant, cocky or boastful and all three of these are negative to your reputation and could cause others to dislike you. Doubting yourself will have a negative effect on your initiative and completing of tasks. It will debilitate your confidence and cause you to have too much humility, which will cause you to project that you are shy or mouse like. Never allow yourself to become timid. Always display the needed amount of confidence.

Never stop planning; you must constantly plan or revise existing plans all the way to your goals. Always evaluate your progress and your efforts to achieve said progress. Make the needed changes to accomplish your tasks. Keep your mind positive to help you. Stay as organized as possible so preparation is always easy to accomplish. **You should plan all the way to your goals**. After you accomplish your goal, think of ways you could have been more effective accomplishing it.

Windows of opportunity; Always practice being patient. Being in a rush has similar negative effects on one as being angry or mad. It causes frustration. It causes your thoughts to be out of control and unfocused. Windows of opportunity don't have a hype man to announce their presence. One must be alert and patiently waiting for them to display themselves. They are not always obvious or in plain sight. One must learn to read between the lines, almost feel their existence before they show themselves. You will get better with practice, so stay positive and be calm. Let the faith you possess show in your demeanor and actions.

Stunting; the art of getting someone's attention and forcing them to notice you in a predetermined light is a science. Stunting can cause negative and positive outcomes. Any stunt performed must be planned and thought out carefully to eliminate any possibility of the stunt causing any negative circumstances. Stunts should elevate your status. They should be used to illuminate a cause or circumstance. They are effective in raising the awareness of something. A stunt must be carefully planned to not cause injury, damage to one's reputation or possibly break one of God's or man's laws.

Beware the *No man* and the *Yes man*. No men and Yes men are polar opposites; however they have a lot in common. They can both be very disruptive to an inner circle or a team. There is no way to gauge what they really feel about something, because their emotions always give their opinions and not their logical minds. They both can destroy an effort in one statement or gesture. The Yes man is the quintessential kiss ass/brown noser. They will do or say anything to impress their person of interest. Usually a supervisor, a love interest or someone they want something from.

The No man is the exact opposite. They are the quintessential hater. They will do anything they can to suppress, silence, embarrass or disgrace and/ or hurt in some cases their person of interest. Usually a rival co-worker, a supervisor they can't stand. The spouse or loved one of someone they are in love with or just someone they are envious or jealous of.

Anything these two say to you, (if you are their person of interest and are aware of it) you must take with a grain of salt. Always asking yourself these questions when dealing with them:

- What is their motivation?
- What do they have to gain?
- Did it sound like they did their research before answering?
- What is their body language doing and does it reflect the words that are coming out of their mouth.

Too make a long story short you can't trust either one of these characters and they should never be allowed in your inner circle and eliminated from a team, ASAP. While you are stuck with them turn their extreme personalities into a positive and send them to do your dirty work. Both will get their hands dirty over their person of interest.

It is always a wise and intelligent habit to attempt to reinvent yourself every now and then, as needed. You need to try and keep your competition and enemies guessing or confused when they are trying to guess what your next move might be or why you took a certain approach to a problem's solution. Reinventing yourself will allow you to see other personalities of the people closest to you and around you. This is important while you are in the neutral phase. You need to let them show you via their actions and body language how loyal they would be and are to you. Pay close attention to their subtle mood changes, facial expressions and conversation.

Before you can commit to any one professionally or personally you must know their opinions on everything, you care about. Try and get an accurate idea of how much you have in common with them. This study will allow you to see exactly what they bring to the table and who they are to you as a person, friend, business associate, lover or coworker. Always be unpredictable. Always have a new and fresh approach to common and daily tasks. This is good so they can't see your actions until you are ready to reveal yourself. Telegraphing your actions and thoughts can cause competition and or jealousy.

Learn as much as you can about your job. Constantly improve your knowledge base about performing your jobs tasks. The accumulation of knowledge is a good foundation to achieve success in any position. Do the best quality work you can. This benefits you in so many areas. Work extra when you have the time.

This is something that needs to be done wisely. People take advantage of hard workers. So pick and choose your times to excel or go the extra mile. Your most important task, is to understand your supervisor's personality as much and as quickly as possible. Some supervisors will use a good worker and take advantage of their good nature and work ethic. One must determine with wisdom what extra work will actually benefit them prior to volunteering, requesting or accepting extra work.

In every industry, unexpected problems can and will develop and arise, that need immediate attention. This is a window of opportunity for you. Pay attention to the people that solve problems efficiently. Always stay alert so when you notice some of these problems, you can take your time and think of wise, logical and intelligent ways to develop several solutions for them, before you acknowledge the problem publicly. Always give them as many as you feel are needed, educated options for the problems' solution.

It is always good to find problems, but if you don't have solutions for the problems you discover, sooner or later people will not want to hear about them, because there is no solution at the time. Meanwhile, if you develop a reputation of being a problem solver, people will seek you out to help them solve their problems that they encounter. This will give one job security and additional competence in performing their jobs daily tasks. Developing a problem solver mentality, will boost your confidence, boost your coworker's confidence in you and get you noticed by people with higher company positions than you.

This also leads to developing a strong reputation which is great for advancement. Seek out and be a part of productive teams by using your wisdom and problem solving skills to help you and your team succeed.

Almost like clockwork, once you start to gain confidence, respect and a good working reputation, someone will become envious and or jealous. Always be aware of who is feeling negative emotions for you. When they reveal themselves, and they will, one must move with cunning and caution to avoid traps and pitfalls created by these individuals.

f the potential enemy does not know you are aware of them, then use this to your advantage. This gives you a form of stealth mode to determine your best place to attack or defend against the enemies advance. Crush all enemies totally. If you don't, they will continue to develop negative efforts against you. If you can't crush them then form a plan to keep them at bay and away from you, your inner circle and your weaknesses. You must survive every battle fought. One must constantly weigh actions prior to committing them to determine any potential negative fallout. Sometime you may need to use another enemy as a mark or fall guy. You can kill two hater's efforts with one stone.

I could mention this next topic several times more and it wouldn't be overdone. Always spend less money than your income in that pay period. A good rule of thumb is always try to earn 2 times the amount you spend. The idea and eventual goal is to increase this amount to maybe 4 and 5 times as you become more financially stable.

- Always pay yourself first before paying anyone else.
- If your budget is tight, force yourself to save a particular amount every pay period. Do not vary from this habit.
- Do without some of your luxuries or entertainment that cost money if you need too. This is a time when negative influence is really your worst enemy.
- Do not listen to others when doing this. It would be better to not even mention it. Some people, if they know you have money, they will make it their business to try and get a hand in your pocket, to

get some of your money. They don't have a need to know anything about your money. Keep it that way.

Another good habit to create for yourself is never paying off debt with your savings. Never spend your savings unless in an emergency situation. Work overtime, do without a luxury or take on a second job. One of my spending philosophies is credit should only be used for houses and emergencies and maybe a vehicle, if you can't afford to buy it cash.

Credit is not for your benefit as the borrower. It only truly benefits the entity loaning the funds out. If I can't buy it cash I can't afford it. If you are in a position where you must use credit for a purchase, pay off the debt every month or entirely as soon as possible. The faster you pay them off, the better. This way hopefully, done properly you will spend less by avoiding some of the interest. Your goal is to be debt free. Again buy anything you can, cash and if you can't buy it cash, save the money up for it. Avoid using credit unless it's an emergency. Get a second job or take on a multi-level marketing business if need be, to accomplish your goal of becoming debt free. Proper and wise utilization of your productive hours is essential to maintaining a sound financial base.

Technology has made life easier and put's one at more financial risk, due to hackers that are internet thieves. Because of this I have mixed emotions about using an automatic payroll deduction. I am old school and prefer to hold my cash myself in a safe manner. However if you are as lazy as I am about paying bills this is a necessary evil. Having an electronic accountant to take care of expenses on time will keep your credit rating stable and shows that creditors (whom you shouldn't give a damn about, unless purchasing a home) will be more likely to finance that big ticket item.

Some people plan properly or are lucky enough to have a job they actually love. I suggest that if you have a choice always choose a position you enjoy and you will have a much better success at being successful in your chosen field. Also, developing other labors of love would be very beneficial. Sometimes we must develop Ifcome and turn it into income. Working in a field you enjoy will help you spend more time at work and have a better chance of excelling at it.

Let your work quality, positive personality, work ethic and attention to detail capture others attention and admiration. Perfect the act of identifying problems. Make a list of them. Create solutions to these problems. Pick and choose your times to solve problems with wisdom. You don't want to make someone look bad or outshine the wrong person. Play these cards when no one has a clue what to do to solve a certain condition. Be the hero. Make your solutions shine, with you staying as humble as possible.

Invest in yourself over stock market financial products. Playing the stock market in my opinion is a form of gambling. True enough, people have made fortunes in the stock market. By the same token too, people have gotten rich betting and gambling.

I prefer to earn money and putting it in a non-risky account. However if you have the knowledge, understanding and wisdom to be successful in the stock market, I will not hate and say…more power to you and I hope you are successful.

CHAPTER 17

JOB SHOPPING 101

When a recruiter calls you about a job take a few notes. You need to know the location, the cost of living there, the job description, the rate, per diem split and the possibility of overtime work. The recruiter will attempt to get you to commit at that moment. Have him give you a little time to do some research. Don't let them bully you, Make them wait in a very professional manner. Be polite and courteous all of the time.

Look at the demographics of the city. Check motel cost; determine how many miles it is from home base for fuel estimations. Once you get all this information seriously consider if this contract is worth it.

Don't get emotional when making these kinds of decisions. You must maintain a stable and calm mind in all contract negotiations. I don't care how much the rate is, never show weakness by being emotional. Call the recruiter back and give him your decision. Question the recruiter about a phone interview with the client. Once you have the recruiter's word about a phone interview, go to the client's website and study the company. Take notes and make sure you make a list of 10-15 very good questions to ask the interviewer. This shows initiative and interest in the client company. Always avoid in person interviews. My reasoning is, why spend your own money on gas, food and motel to go visit a company that may decide they don't like you for non-professional reasons.

This has actually happened to me. I mean this is a form of gambling and gambling hard earned money is never wise and If the client decides yes, and the recruiter gives you the heads up that your submittal has been accepted, you should find a motel you like and book your reservation for at least a week to get the best rate possible. Motels are usually willing to drop their daily rate and give you a low special one if you let them know you will be a guest for a work contract and there is no end date.

Once you are there for a little while you can start looking for temporary living to cut your expenses. If you want to get a small place, as in one bedroom apartment, efficiency or maybe a roommate scenario there are a few things to consider:

- Never commit to a binding lease ever, unless you like giving money away. You have no idea how long your contract will last so signing anything over a 3 month lease is very risky. If the job ends as you know, legally you could be still responsible for the financial obligation of the lease if you commit to a normal rental agreement. Always attempt to get a month to month lease or an early move out clause for end of job reasons.
- A roommate scenario can be your best route however that always depends on who you choose for a roommate. Remember that Bridget Fonda movie ***Single White Female***? There is no rush. Get to know this person very well before committing to move in with them. This is supposed to be a benefit not some sort burden.

Job shopping can give one an illusion of being financially secure and can and always give a person a quick financial recovery when the funds become low. You should build your emergency fund to an amount equal to three months of income. That's like 12-15 paychecks before even considering the concept of relaxing on your savings effort.

You really need your money divided up into four categories:

- Working capital for bills
- Your spending money
- Your emergency fund, and
- Your nest egg for vacations, home purchase and retirement.

Job Droughts...Job droughts are the period of time one is unemployed trying to secure another contract. After a job drought, once a Shopper secures a contract he can recover relatively quickly to a stable financial level. The problem with this is money can go out faster than it comes in depending on one's debt structure. One must remember that this industry is not just employment, one must think like it is a business, because it is. It may only have one employee but it is still a business. So one must never get comfortable. One must constantly live like they are currently in a job drought, whether they are or not. Budget is the word to make your best friend.

Security Clearances...Some positions a Job Shopper will be submitted on will require one of the following security clearances. A security clearance is a status granted to some individuals allowing them access to classified information, material and restricted areas. A thorough background check is required to be approved for any of these clearances. Anyone with access to classified data requires a clearance at or higher than the level at which the data is classified. For this reason, security clearances are required for a wide range of jobs, from senior management to janitorial.

There are three levels of clearance

- Confidential - This level of clearance will grant certain individuals the right to access designated and classified information up to confidential level on a need-to-know basis. This is hierarchically the first security clearance to get, typically requiring a few weeks to a few months of investigation. A Confidential clearance requires a National Agency Check with Law and Credit (N.A.C.L.C.) investigation which dates back 7 years on the subject's record and must be renewed (with another investigation) every 15 years.
- Secret - This level of clearance will grant certain individuals the right to access designated and classified information up to Secret level on a need- to-know basis. A Secret clearance, also known as Collateral Secret or Ordinary Secret, requires a few months to a year to investigate, depending on the individual's background.

Some instances wherein individuals would take longer than normal to be investigated are many past residences, having residences in foreign countries, having relatives outside the United States, or significant ties with non-United States citizens.

Unpaid bills as well as criminal charges will more than likely disqualify an applicant for approval. However, a bankruptcy will be evaluated on a case-by-case basis and is not an automatic disqualifier. Poor financial history is the number-one cause of rejection, and foreign activities and a criminal record are also common causes for disqualification. A Secret clearance requires an N.A.C.L.C., and a Credit investigation; it must also be re-investigated every 10 years.

- Top Secret - This level of clearance will grant certain individuals the right to access all designated and classified information on a need-to-know basis. Top Secret is a more stringent clearance. A Top Secret, or "TS", clearance is often given as the result of a Single Scope Background Investigation, or SSBI. Top Secret clearances, in general, afford one access to data that affects national security, counterterrorism, counterintelligence, or other highly sensitive data. There are far fewer individuals with Top Secret clearances than Secret clearances. A Top Secret clearance can take as few as 3 to 6 months to acquire, but often it takes 6 to 18 months. The SSBI must be reinvestigated every 5 years. In order to receive a Top Secret clearance, all candidates must pass an oral interview.

According to a 2010 ***Washington Post*** article, 854,000 Americans had top-secret clearances; almost one-third of them worked for private companies, rather than for the U.S. government. Jobs that require a security clearance can be found either as positions working for the federal government or as federal contractors.

Lately, more clearance type jobs are being outsourced to contractors. Clearances will have an effect on your life as far as who you can socialize with, date, your relatives, your past, present and future personal life. At some levels you will be watched and reported on about your daily activities. This is to ensure there is no espionage or unpatriotic behavior.

The vetting process for a security clearance is usually undertaken only when someone is hired or transferred into a position that requires access to classified information. The employee is typically fingerprinted and asked to provide information about themselves. This becomes a starting point for an investigation into the candidate's suitability. The process has been streamlined and now requires the person who needs clearance to input the information online using e-QIP; five days are allowed for data input. Having the older paper form can be helpful for collecting and organizing the information in advance.

CHAPTER 18

THE RECRUITERS

Most recruiters know very little about any job. They memorize buzz words in an attempt to speak intellectually. Sometimes I wonder from the questions they ask have they even read my resume. A recruiter thinks you are a dime a dozen and will treat you accordingly. It is a pimp and hoe mentality, don't get it twisted....and you already know who will get screwed if they aren't careful and wise. The Shopper.

A Recruiter will often test you to see how green or ignorant you are to the business. Recruiters will try anything with you they think they can get you to do, cuss you out if you don't; seriously.

I accepted a position once in Fort Wayne Indiana, my home town. A recruiter called me the next day. He talked me into listening to his pitch about his job. He said he had a position that was perfect for my skill set. I replied I just accepted a position. He wouldn't take no for an answer and just to appease him I told him to go ahead and tell me about it.

The really crazy thing it turned out was the position he supposedly had was the one I just accepted. I quickly told him that I was already hired for that position and had signed the contract and everything. This seemed to excite him some. He said no worries just cut the shop off that already got you the job and let him represent me. I thought about it. I have nothing to gain and a contract to lose. I told him I wasn't willing to change at this late stage and he snapped. This ass hole started cussing me out like crazy.

I was in a good mood and decided to keep myself in good spirits. I put the phone down. I went upstairs to use the bathroom. I came back down stairs and put the phone to my ear and he was still going off and had no idea I even put the phone down. When he finally calmed down we ended the phone call. Never spoke to him again. Ironically I told my supervisor at the client company months later this story and he said you are lucky you didn't do that. I would have thrown your resume in the trash and hired someone else. Now ain't that some shit.

Recruiters will on occasion engage in back door deals with companies that aren't in the Shopper's best interest. A recruiter will lie to you, so take anything they say with a grain of salt. Don't be afraid to ask a question more than once if that answer is important to you. Don't be afraid or nervous period. They are only really loyal to the client customer, but will say anything to the shopper to cause them to feel that the recruiters has the back of the shopper. It is all a deception to get you to trust them If they ever say trust me, do the opposite.

If the customer screws the shopper over, the recruiter will always side with the customer. The deals they strike the shopper never sees. They will use intimidation and manipulation to coerce a shopper into doing what that recruiter wants regardless of what negativity the shopper inherits. They will ask ridiculous questions just to see if they can catch a shopper slipping.

In the recruiter's mind the shopper is expendable, however the customer is not. They will waste a shopper's time. If they don't have a job, end the phone call. The recruiter is not your friend. There is no benefit from having social conversations with them. Be polite and courteous, but beyond that, keep it business. If they are overly nice, and they don't have a job, they want something from you and usually that is information about the company you are currently working at, which they don't have a need to know. Again if they don't have a job for you....get off the phone. They will flirt with the opposite sex and possibly talk about dates even. Don't ever feel pressure to tell a recruiter information about the company you are working at.

I once had a recruiter call me early in the morning and pretend to be my girlfriend. So never just volunteer any information that they don't need to know. These are all information tactics. The only subjects that should be spoken about are jobs, getting them an updated resume or referring another shopper to them. Anything else is a waste of time.

I was in an unexpected drought, (all are usually unexpected), and a group of recruiters came to me and rewrote my resume with specific buzz words to get their client to bite. Pause.... If some of these individuals would lie to their client and the client is the priority, how much do they value the shopper?

I have heard stories of people traveling all the way across the country on their own expense for a contract, while unemployed or recently quit their previous position for this contract and arrive and there is no job. The last few years, recruiters have been calling and I can't understand a word they are saying. I call it the foreign invasion. Yo Gubna decided that non-citizens needed jobs in this country more than natural-born or naturalized citizens. I was taught to take care of home first. I guess not everyone feels that way.

My issue with this is if I can't understand someone and we are talking about my life, my bills getting paid and where I am going to be living the next few months and they can barely understand me as well, how much can I trust or bank on the conversation? Well some say we need to elect people in office that will do a good job. They often ask me did I vote. I say hell no and this is why. Why should I waste my time when I could be doing something that benefits me or someone else? Voting for someone that will give our jobs to foreigners and go as far as let them work our jobs from a foreign country when we have unemployed and homeless people in this country.

Vote for someone that spends their whole day figuring out how to put more money in their pockets, argue their enemies legislation off the table whether it is good for the people or not and nine out of ten times forget about the people like me once they get in office. And as far as the President........The Electoral College. Nuff said.

I worked for a European owned Texas Airline manufacturer and they had more Asian Indians (non U S citizens) working than "white" employees born in this country let alone any other race in the engineering department. This country seems just like Babylon AK the whore; everybody can get a piece of the American Dream except some so-called Americans.

So instead of voting I think I will write another book to help people or coach a kids sports team, teach unemployed, unskilled laborers Pro-Engineer or make a hip hop record. It doesn't matter as long as it's positive and productive.

Voting is a waste of my time. Moving on. Like Wal-Mart did to the Mom and Pop stores, a great deal of industries and major corporations are swallowing the small ones. The agencies that employ recruiters are owned by the same holding company a lot of times. I was in a terrible situation. My health was being affected by the work environment I was in.

As I stated earlier no job is worth your health or life. You can get another job, you can't get another life. I negotiated another position and left. Now my recruiter knew everything I was going through from start to finish. A couple contracts in the future I was contacted by another firm and about the time I received the electronic contract, a recruiter mentioned to me that the company I mentioned earlier was a sibling company and they weren't going to hold against me what happened at the job that I chose health over income. Two lessons here, recruiters don't give a damn about you and be careful what bridge you burn if you feel the need to burn one.

I just got off the phone with a recruiter. I just can't trust those individuals. This guy asked me where I was working. I asked him why did he have a need to know and his answer had nothing to do with our conversation at that moment. He asked me my salary and I asked him why he had a need to know and he changed the subject. That is very slimy to me. I will never trust these people. They are something like a pimp and they consider us something like a *whore*. So you can easily understand why you need to feed these people with long handled spoons.

CHAPTER 19

THE CLIENT COMPANY

The client company is the equivalent or the exact same entity as your customer if you owned a store. The difference is they pay the job shop and the job shop pays you. The client companies are the source of the money flow. So because you are the type that doesn't bite the hand that feeds them you will never ever under any circumstances piss off the client company.

I don't really care what they do. You must develop some scar tissue and not show any sensitivity. As long as it doesn't affect your life or business negatively have an "I don't give a damn attitude" about everything except your work quality and reputation. If you show emotion you give away a weakness and an enemy that you may not be aware of can attack you.

Keep your personal opinions and feelings separate. Remember never let them know what you are thinking unless it will benefit your team. I realize this can be difficult at times. The feeling of disrespect is hard to shake, but one must. Your personal life demands it and depends on it. Don't get me wrong, I am not saying grin real big and do a shuffle dance, Mr. Bo-jangles. Just make your money in a mindset that should produce in a manner that benefits everyone involved and don't take anything personal. Remember it is all business.

Potential Bosses

I have had so many different personality types in supervisors and I had to learn on the fly how to deal with them. From racist, to lame ducks, to average, to positive and intellectually sound leaders. You could possibly get any one of the negative characters in <u>Chapter one</u> or possibly any of the positive people in <u>Chapter two</u>.

If you get one of the negative types, you may want to consider getting another job. Sometimes these individuals can make your life a living hell. I wouldn't be too concerned about burning a bridge in this case. If they are one of the personalities described in Chapter one, they most likely wouldn't re-hire you anyway. I decided to dive in deeper and break down the supervisor, so once you recognize yours for who they are you can act in a manner that is in your best interest. From my experience I came up with 8 different supervisor personality types. These personality types only describe the person's hard wiring. They still have the ability to think, reason and react. So just because you can put them in one of these categories doesn't mean you know for a fact what they are thinking. Stay humble.

The first one I call the ***Mentor***. The Mentor Is the perfect teacher and advisor. They will invest time into you, push you to become better and will let you go with no problem when it's time to move on.

The second one I call the ***Parent***. They want to nurture their people forever. They will invest time into you and push you to become better but will want to keep you in their group as their employee forever.

Number three I call ***Freddie Kruger***. Why? Because this supervisor is a nightmare on any street. They will invest time into you but will block your progress whenever possible and will let you go with no problem when it's time to move on.

Number four I call ***Correctional Officer***, because they give you a feeling of incarceration every time you come to work. They will invest time into you, but will block your progress and will want to keep you in their group without a promotion forever.

I call number five the ***Psychic*** because they always seem to know what to do. Never invests any time with you, but somehow pushes you to become better and will let you with no problem go when it's time to move on.

Your ***God Parent*** is number six. They don't invest any time with you but still push you to become better and want to keep you in their group without a promotion forever.

Number seven I call ***Hitler,*** because it's a matter of time before you get burned. They won't invest any time with you, will block your progress and will let you go with no problem when it's time to move on.

Number eight I call **Satan** because you are in a form of hell working for them. They will not invest any time with you but will block your progress and will want to keep you in their group without a promotion forever.

Supervisors are always right, even when they are wrong. No dispute, debate or argument is worth losing your contract over, so if it doesn't make you look like a fool, just go along with it. It's their money and if you want to continue getting your cut....again just go along with it.

I have a supervisor presently that will ask me a question and walk away before I finish my answer; like right in the middle of it. He will publicly blame me for something that he knows for a fact was mostly out of my control. He will tell me to listen to one of his right hands and knows that right hand rarely listens to him. He will then get mad at me like it's my fault.

It doesn't matter as long as he keeps signing my time sheet and I continue getting paid. Laugh at them all the way to your bank so to speak, but never disrespect your supervisor even if he deserves it. I told a co-worker the other day something. He said our supervisor gave him a task that wouldn't work and was a waste of time and money. Guess what I told him. I said do the job exactly like our supervisor requested it, but in addition to that effort do it the way you feel is right and submit it to our supervisor after the fact as if the supervisor inspired the concept and the shopper just acted on the inspiration of the supervisor. You don't care about credit. You care about continuing to get paid and keeping your likeability factor high and your professional respect level higher.

Direct Employees...Some direct employees have done the same job for so many years that they get a sense of tunnel vision, since they have no idea of how other companies deal with the same type of design issue. They do it the same way for so long they seem to feel there can't be a better way to achieve the same goal. They tend to get very comfortable and often become arrogant and extremely defensive in some cases about the way they approach a design task. Some develop huge egos.

When a job shopper gets hired, the direct employee, depending on how insecure the employee is, will tend to have a negative disposition toward the job shopper. They seem to get a bit of a God complex whether they sign your time sheet or not.

If you spend your life in one room you would know everything about that room. They seem to think everyone else should know everything they know and will lose patience with a shopper because they don't have the patience to explain something thoroughly in a non-condescending manner. The problem with these people is they tend to think because a shopper doesn't know one thing they don't know anything and start being a micro-manager. This makes it extremely difficult to work with an individual like this.

Now imagine being a long way from home. You are at the beginning of a contract and you have invested more money than you have made into the job and you have to work with an individual like this and normally they seem to always have the boss's ear. That's stress. No other way to describe it especially if you are coming out of a job drought and have been living on unemployment for several months.

Some direct employees use this isolated knowledge as a weapon to dominate shoppers when they can't afford to lose the job and have gambled a lot of money on taking the job. I have learned from experience to not volunteer the fact that I am not aware of something or never learned it. I try to never ever tell them any personal business even if they ask a personal question. Politely tell them that you don't mix business with pleasure and your personal life is personal for obvious reasons. A great deal of direct employees are very insecure and any potential threat in their eyes is a potential war waiting to happen. The direct employee's response to this is to get defensive and start plotting offensive strategies that may lead to your down fall. It will almost always be used against you by an enemy. So when I realize I don't know something I speak very little about it and go study it as quick as possible.

Potential Coworkers

Note: The beautiful thing about having a very wise editor is the conversations with her. We had quite a few really poignant conversations about this manuscript. It really helped to improve it greatly in my opinion. After one of these conversations I decided to add this next section to help an employee understand his co-workers in a more efficient manner.

They are—

- The Ultimate Team Player
- The Boss Wanna Be
- The Prankster
- The Social Engineer
- The Stuffed Shirt
- The Know-it-all
- The Spy
- The Traitor

Please keep in mind, everyone has preferences and has the freedom to make choices in life. The explanations I am outlining in this chapter are not stereotypes, but an example of several personality types that one may encounter. As with the **Bosses** I broke this section down in a similar manner.

The ***Ultimate Team Player*** is as close to the perfect co-worker in my opinion as possible. This person is truly a team player. They are concerned about the way other workers feel. They realize that attitudes will affect how others feel about them. They seek out problems and solve them. They seem to feel a need to fix things that are broken or need an improvement. They are very aware of their circumstances and environment and tend to want to set positive examples for their fellow co-workers. They have a tendency to take their work extremely seriously. They will speak their mind and are almost never are the two faced type.

They have no problem helping others or mentoring younger or inexperienced co-workers. They tend to avoid drama and negative situations and actually consider the worst case scenario before acting.

They are reluctant to take sides and try to stay neutral to avoid conflicts. They avoid participating in gossip, but may listen. They tend to have their priorities in proper order and possess the "it's only a job" attitude. They consider their personal life to be far more important than their professional life. They may or may not make friends on the job. They don't seem to care if that happens or not. They usually prefer to not let their personal interests and life become common knowledge in the office. They keep both lives separate. If this character becomes a supervisor they will most likely evolve into the ***Mentor*** boss personality.

The ***Boss Wanna-Be*** is very possibly a good candidate for an ulcer, as they are obsessed with their career and will make sacrifices in their personal life in order for, in their opinion, be more effective at work.

The Boss Wanna-Be can and will take work way too seriously. They are a team player, but seem to seek out friends at work as if they were looking for a personal friend. They have the BFF at work complex. They will want to do everything with their BFF or group of BFF's.

They are concerned about the way other workers feel and especially their work friends. They enjoy and relish being a hero and jump at the chance to solve problems. They strive to be a leader and they try to set positive examples.

They will speak their minds as long as it won't hurt or have a negative effect on their job, BFF or reputation. They aren't two faced, intentionally, usually but may accidently throw someone under the bus. Now if it's them or you, it depends on the morality of the person.

They generally will help other employees if it isn't a career gamble. They usually won't participate in gossip, but may listen and laugh. The down side to this person is they can be very selfish at times times due to certain loyalties. And last but very important is to understand and accept that they maybe a brown noser. Which, is never a bad thing as long as the Boss Wanna-Be doesn't cause negativity for themselves or someone else.

The Boss Wanna-Be may have a tendency to, as the saying goes, burn the candle at both ends. If this character becomes a supervisor they will most likely evolve into the *Parent* supervisor personality.

The *Prankster* is not a team player unless they find some enjoyment from it and or benefit. They may be the office clown, comedian or instigator. Some have a tendency to be annoying, on purpose, and may cause work related problems. For their amusement they may play co-workers against each other.

They will at times speak their minds without empathy for the person they are talking too. Some can be very two faced, while some will help other employees. They are reluctant to take sides and often try to stay neutral. They seem to only make alliances when there is a benefit. They are aware that attitudes will effect how others feel about them.

The Prankster has an "it's only a job" attitude. They usually have several sexual relationships at a time. They may or may not make friends on the job and don't care if they do or not. They seem to have a good understanding of their fellow employee's personalities. They are usually not two faced, because they don't care what anyone thinks about them. They tend to understands their fellow employees and spend time paying attention to them. The Prankster realizes that attitudes will effect how others feel about them. If this character becomes a supervisor they will most likely evolve into the *Psychic* supervisor personality.

The ***Social Engineer*** is not per se a team player, but may have their finger on the pulse of the office. They are often non-empathetic, very nosey and attempt to be controlling. They can be extremely annoying and may cause work related problems. They often play co-workers against each other.

They can be the office clown and appear to be a Prankster at times, however lacking the realness or depth of a Prankster. They often speak their minds and can be two faced. They may participate in gossip or even start rumors. They will help fellow employees when there appears to be some benefit for them. They should not be counted on to solve problems, often lacking the focus to concentrate. They can become very obsessed with the socials life of their job. Their main mission on the job is to set up networks and alliances.

They tend to make friends very easily. They can be extremely self-centered and selfish at times; often due to certain loyalties. They are often willing to put fellow employees down in order to look good. They can also be considered a brown noser. If this character becomes a supervisor they will most likely evolve into the ***God Parent*** supervisor personality.

The ***Stuffed Shirt*** is often a problem solver. They tend to think they are setting a good example, however are covertly or with our realizing it, trying to manipulate co-workers. They often tend to negative responses and opinions.

They will be a team player but only playing by their own rules. Some, for negative or positive reasons, tend to be concerned about how other co-workers feel. At times they can be very two faced and will often work against or sabotage other employees' efforts. They understand that life outside of the job is more important than life on the job. They can and will spread negative gossip.

Constant complaining is something they may often tend to do. The Stuffed Shirt loves to use the word no as an answer to most requests and may or may not make friends on the job. They really don't care. They tend to understand their fellow employees and avoid taking sides and seem to try to stay neutral to avoid conflicts, because they realize that attitudes will effect how others feel about or act towards them. If this character becomes a supervisor they will most likely evolve into the ***Freddie Kruger*** supervisor personality.

The ***Know-it-all*** tends to be a team player. They are concerned about the way other workers feel about job related issues. They want to solve problems and most of the times try to set positive example. They can and will take work way too seriously and often destroy relationships and their personal lives for the job.

This person can be two faced and should not be trusted. They will work against and or sabotage other employees and their efforts. They appreciate gossip and have no problem spreading some, whether good or bad. They hate foul language and attempt to sensor other employees. They are usually constant gossipers and complainers and want to push their ideals and beliefs on you. They often are haters and love to use the word no as an answer to most request from co-workers. The Know it all is usually not two faced and will speak their minds. They will help other employees and have a willingness to solve problems. They seem to believe that they know more about most topics than most people. They can be extremely condescending and have a tendency to dismiss the opinion of others whether they or right or wrong. If this character becomes a supervisor they will most likely evolve into the ***Correctional Officer*** supervisor.

The ***Spy*** may or may not be a team player. They may have many alliances or possibly have none. They will act any way they deem fit to accomplish a goal. They can be annoying and may stage or cause work related problems. Some will make an art form out of playing co-workers against each other.

They have no issue working against or sabotaging other employees' projects, reputation and work ethic. Once identified, they can never be trusted under any circumstance. They are definatly two faced. They enjoy spreading negative gossip and will constantly complain about most things. They seem to enjoy denying coworkers assistance. They almost always have an" it's only a job" attitude (personal life is more important). They don't care if they make friends on the job.

They take time to study fellow employee's personalities. Because the Spy has many alliances, they can never publicly take sides and tend to instigate, but shy away from actual involvement in conflicts in the work place.

The Spy realizes that attitudes will effect how others feel about them and strives to maintain minimum visability. If this character becomes a supervisor they will most likely evolve into the *Hitler* supervisor personality.

The *Traitor* may front like a team player, however always has an alterior motive. They give concern about the way other workers are feeling in order to use the knowledge against them. They will create job chaos and create negative vibes. They are in most cases extremely two faced. They take pleasure in working against and or sabotaging other employees and their efforts.

They enjoy starting and spreading negative gossip either true or false. They always have gripes or complaints. They enjoy causing chaos and denying fellow coworkers assistance. They can be at times almost obsessed with their career or job.

They like to make friends on the job, but will turn on them in a heartbeat. They tend to be selfish at times due to certain loyalties. They enjoy being the one that shines. They are excellent ass kissers. If this character becomes a supervisor they will most likely evolve into the *Satan* supervisor personality.

CHAPTER 20

FINANCIAL BUSINESS

What is Job Shopping specifically?

Have you ever worked for a temporary agency before?

It is essentially the same thing however, because you are specialized you usually are needed a lot longer and of course your wages are a lot higher.

A shopper usually has a home somewhere else and you have to pay for your existence in two places. Per Diem helps the shopper a lot. Always ask for it. Wages differ just like in the regular work force. I have heard of some shoppers making over $100.00 per hour. Usually that is some electrical, software/hardware or a number cruncher as I call them, basically a math whiz.

Companies will pay a vast range of salaries for the same type of position and some companies are willing to pay more than others. A recruiter will ask you what rate you expect. Never state a rate to a recruiter. This is a way of eliminating someone that wants in the recruiters mind too much salary or let them know they can pay the shopper a low wage and make more profit for them and their agency. Always ask what will the client pay. The recruiter knows this already. They gave him a salary range for the position.

Always ask approximately how long they expect the contract to last. A recruiter usually has enough information to give you a good guess of how long the job should last, but it is only a guess and there are no guarantees of job length in job shopping. They can guess by how long their people have stayed or lasted or what the company's purchase order allows.

In Job Shopping there is no so called job security. Your bank account is your job security, literally. The more money you have the more stability and freedom you have. You need to constantly add to it and not risk it on a gamble. Most important never invest your money for a job that is not definite. This can hurt a budget. If an employer wants you to invest money in this manner you should move forward with caution. If however, you are extremely confident that you can acquire the position then do the math and consider going. Keep in mind this gives the client customer a chance to last minute judge you and possibly negatively. Keep in mind people aren't always good people and are not always what they seem to be at first glance.

Looks can be deceiving as well as voices. Here are two examples of voices. I was living down in New Orleans. Every now and then for extra money at times in my life I would moon light as a club, party or wedding reception DJ. I inquired about a DJ job with a local West Bank DJ company. I spoke to the owner on the phone and we got along great in the conversation and I went away from the phone interview feeling very confident and assumed he was black as well. The day came and I went in to the office for a face to face interview. The owner came out and we both gave each other a bit of the "oh shit he's white/black" look. I remember we came away from the meeting respecting each other but there wasn't any more banter or comradery in our conversation and I never worked for that company. Can't remember why but I never did.

Also, in my hometown of Fort Wayne Indiana, I was a local on air personality on a cable radio RnB station called COOL Radio, 99.7 FM (All the radio you will ever need). I remember at least once every show I would do, one or two people would ask me if I was white. Imagine that.

So my whole point is before you go getting all confident and rushing to go to an in person interview stop, think and use the best wisdom you have before you go gambling money on a job that is not promised to you.

One job in particular I remember because it was a get-paid-every-other-week type. Every week is so much nicer, but sometimes you gotta do what you gotta do. So I had to work an entire month without any income. This is another instance when budgeting properly on the previous contract pays dividends on the new one.

A recruiter once told me after he deposited my first check. He told me yeah Dave; it's time to party now. I was almost offended, because I understand the trap in his words. He most likely had no idea how terribly wrong he did me at that moment and most people wouldn't notice it. That kind of communication in the ear of the naive job shopper is potentially devastating. If one immediately goes out to party without thinking about where his money needs to go he could have problems.

Before anything is paid or done, pull 25% out, place it in an account that doesn't have ATM access or checks attached to it and forget about it, literally. Take 25% and pay as much of your household bills as possible. Take 25% and stash it locally for your on the road expenses. The balance is there to cover anything extra like a car repair, help on the household bills or any other financial emergency that might pop up. If you don't need to spend this money forget about it. It will come in handy when the unforeseen financial emergency pops up.

Now I know some of you are doing your math and are feeling like this is an all work and no fun type of scenario. The 25% you put aside for your road expenses doubles as your fun budget. Once you pay your motel, gas and food expenses whatever is left can be blown. Now you can go to the club, the bar, the strip joint or the casino and possess the confidence that you are acting responsibly no matter how much of your chump change you lose, blow or give away.

Never put yourself in harm's way for a paycheck, safety is a priority. Let's face it, without your health it can be very difficult to work. If you can't work you don't make money. It doesn't take a rocket engineer to figure out that paying attention to the clients PPE (Personal Protection Equipment) regulations and other standard operating procedures is crucial. One must be aware of the environment and the potential hazards and dangerous scenarios and conditions and always wear safety shoes, eye goggles, ear protection, proper coats and gloves etc., whenever required by the client.

Job droughts happen all the time. One must always be aware that one could happen at any time. One unexpected layoff can send a Job Shopper's life spiraling out of control if he or she does not plan for them when they are doing well. Job Shopping is like a sine or cosine wave for you Trig wizards. There are high points and low ones. It's literally feast or famine. When you are doing well act like you are not. Budget like crazy. Remember the 25% that I told you to forget about. Well during a job drought you will remember it and be thankful you forgot about it.

In an ideal world this is retirement funds or that well needed vacation, but in all reality most likely at times it will be a CYA fund (cover your ass fund) type of financial insurance policy.

Never take tax or withholding advice from anyone other than an accountant or a tax professional. This is because he is constantly paying attention to the tax laws and studies how one can pay the least amount of taxes or screw up and pay a hell of a lot more. A shopper gave me some terrible advice one day (when I was just getting started). I was on my very first contract and I was still very naïve (I wish I had this book then) He told me that I could change the amount of taxes being taken out of my check whenever I wanted too. I had no clue I had the right and access to do this.

The downside is taxes still have to be paid, and it is always easier to pay them out of your pay check than to write a check later to the I.R.S. This is very similar to filing a 1099 form. What a 1099 does is get you your earnings from a job without any withholdings. No F.I.C.A. No Federal, local or state tax being withheld what so ever. The upside is either one of these ways of getting paid can bail you out of a tight financial situation. The downside is like I said before it is always easier to pay now than later. With the 1099 you must pay the I.R.S. every 90 days. It would be best to do this with an accountant so you never get behind on your taxes.

Not properly attending to this business could cause you some real drama like the I.R.S. garnishing your pay check or freezing your bank accounts.

Not only that, you can get caught up in a perpetual financial fuck you, messing with them. They can charge you unbelievably high interest rates. So the moral to this story is always pay and file your taxes. Stay on their good side. Always keep your dependent withholdings low and honest and do your best to avoid going exempt or 1099, unless you have a certified public accountant watching your financial back.

Surviving comfortably while on unemployment is something that every job shopper must work towards. This can be difficult especially if the rent or a mortgage payment is a lot. With anything one must reduce debt. One must pay himself first. One must budget like they are unemployed when they are working. Paying attention to the unemployment rates is incredibly important. The Job Shopper must learn to live off that amount of money before the layoff. The concept is maintaining a stable life regardless of employment status. Here is a budget reminder.

- Deposit 25% into an account and forget about it.
- Allot 25% to cover all home cost (mortgage/rent, utilities, and insurances)
- Allot 25% to cover all the job expenses (motel, travel, food) (Extra goes into emergency and self-rewards)
- Use the remaining 25% as an emergency account (pay or pay extra on bills and pay off debt). The main reason to create this account is to give you the confidence that you can budget properly, and that you will always create wealth instead of creating debt.

Keep in mind there is nothing wrong with paying bills in advance. It is a different mindset. I realize this is an aggressive budget, so if you can't do it now, start to adjust your finances to this as quickly as possible. As you payoff credit cards, car loans and other misc credit, it will become doable. Cut up your credit cards. Use debit cards and install the attitude if you can't buy it cash, you can't afford it.

Per Diem is a daily allowance for expenses. It is a specific amount of money an organization gives an individual per day to cover living expenses while traveling for work. Per Diem pay eliminates the need for employees to spend as much time creating expense reports to document amounts spent while travelling on business for reimbursement. Instead, employers pay employees a standard daily rate without regard to the amount actually spent by the employee. In occupations that pay an hourly wage, per diem is calculated as an hourly rate and paid in addition to the contractor's base pay.

The customer billing rate is the amount billed the customer, per hour of labor rendered. It is the hourly rate of the shopper plus the job shop markup, which is usually around 25 to 35 percent. So if the shopper is earning a fifty dollar per hour wage, the billing rate would be approx. sixty five dollars per hour. The customer billing rate is something that has a tremendous effect on the Job Shopper and it can be positive or negative depending on the client customer's circumstances.

On occasion the job shop may bill above the normal mark up. In this case the customer would most likely feel they are over paying for the labor they are getting. This may cause them to look for reasons to eliminate the shopper's position or replace the shop and the shopper for a cheaper billing rate. The billing rate is something that the Shopper may not even need to be aware of, or acknowledge. If he budgets his money properly he couldn't care less about it, for the most part.

When a contract is offered, the job shop will send you out an electronic package containing several documents. The package will contain the employment contract. Make sure you read it, to determine if everything agreed upon verbally is there in writing. The main thing you are looking for is the wage and the per diem amount. Once this is verified you can give a two week notice to your present employer. Never give that notice until you verify your wage in your contract. Also in the package will be an I-9 form to verify citizenship, a W-2 to determine how you will be taxed, a per diem verification form, an intellectual property agreement and various other Job Shop forms and acknowledgements.

The intellectual property agreement should be studied and completely understood. What it says basically is anything you invent while you are under contract with that company is the property of the company. One must make sure that all your inventions are protected prior to accepting employment with the job shop and client company.

A salary advance is a loan from the job shop to the shopper, when they are low on investment funds. Some job shops do it and some don't. After the shopper successfully works anywhere from one to five days, the job shop can give the shopper some of their first check early, in order to cover on site expenses. This is a real benefit after a long job drought.

Always pay attention to the mileage to and from home and the job site as well as from the job site to your temporary housing. Make sure everything make sense before accepting a contract. Mileage can be a very large expense if not planned, investigated and studied properly and thoroughly.

Again, as I said previously, I am not one to tell another person how to eat. I may make a suggestion, but that is about it. A plant based diet will ward off most diseases and keep one away from the doctor's office, the pharmacy and the hospital. However accidents happen that are unforeseen, so purchasing a health insurance package is a good idea if it is feasible for you at the time. Going with the shop, may be convenient, but may not be the best policy for your buck, so I suggest you shop around.

Choosing temporary living can be quite a task when traveling for a new contract position. Always apply the three C's. Cheap, clean and comfortable and they are the highest priorities. One without pets; aka rodents and insects. You want a place in a neighborhood where the smell of urine isn't the dominant aroma.

Sleep is always good, so a place where people go to sleep at night and there is limited nocturnal female attention. In other words; anywhere other than the friendly neighborhood, crack motel. It needs to be a reasonable distance from the job site. Gas and the time it takes to get to work are important factors as well. Cost is always a concern when on the road. You also need to be close enough to get to work in a very short period of time if the client needs you to come in unexpectedly or in urgent moment.

CHAPTER 21

MY EARLY LIFE

I am from a mid-sized, Midwest city known as Fort Wayne Indiana. Best known for being the home town of actresses Shelly Long and Joan Crawford and the city that spawned the Detroit Pistons of the National Basketball Assoc.. Oh, and former Vice President Dan Quayle is from the area as well.

I always told people that Fort Wayne is a wonderful city (voted All American City a few times) to prosper and live comfortably if you weren't Black. An example of that is my senior year in High School I decided to play Baseball. The Baseball Coach told me and a neighborhood friend that he was prejudiced and he would most certainly cut us from the team no matter how good we were. He said this with a very sarcastic condescending tone to his voice and I don't recall him even looking up from his desk at us. We were both pretty good but this really disheartened us both.

I decided not to try out for the team. I didn't want to feel the disappointment of not making a team and went out for track again. At least the coach was fair and color blind and there were no cuts in track. My neighborhood friend did try out. This guy could hit a home run almost anytime he wanted too. After practicing several days with the team he was cut as the coach had promised. You'd think and expect a teacher/coach to help students prosper not send them away hating him their school and their existence in that community.

How disheartening was it? It was the only sport I had any possibility of getting a college scholarship in and that door was shut in my face. I was blatantly average at most things. I was a B student at best in High School and showed descent at best athletic skills. I did have music and acting talent, however my Mother seemed to not want me to pursue that as a career. I mean she would never block me or do anything negative she just wasn't enthusiastic about me doing anything in music.

I was pretty good at piano at ages of 10-12. All the lessons I got were from public school. A's two years straight. What my Mother did do was give me a somewhat sheltered upbringing and taught me to memorize things that were important or she felt I should know all my life. Some of the things she made me memorize were state capitals. I remembered being laughed at when we would walk by homes and children were outside playing and would hear my Mother asking me questions, me answering them as best I could and her scolding me for paying attention to the children playing instead of her. So by the time I was 10 I was much farther ahead academically than most of my peers. All this prepared me for the new school I was going to.

Most of the work seemed easy at times and my Mother maintained her same tactics in the evening. I became the top candidate for the highest academic award given to any student for academic achievement and leadership in my school two years in a row and only lost because I wanted my friend to get it. The award was named after his father and he and I had known each other since we were around 5 years old. I think I gave the best speech of my life the first time because I felt empathy for my friend. I thought that it was cool if the son won the father's award. He was a Jr. as well.

During this period is when I began playing piano. One negative, the better I got, the more people in the neighborhood would dish out homo phobic type of ridicule saying hateful things like only fags play piano. So I quit piano (Dayum wasn't that a stupid move). Anyway about that time desegregation laws started to be implemented and school busing starting. A permanent program to ship inner city children to public schools in the suburbs. None of us wanted to go way out there. To this day I don't understand it. If our schools were inferior then make them academically equal to other schools in the district I would think would be logical. We passed two other high schools on the way to the one they were sending us too.

Hmmm.... This was during a time when gas prices were on the news daily. They were extremely high for the time. It felt so weird being forced to go to a school in areas that we knew no one and no one cared about us there. That was a time when one or two black guys could get beat up or worse for walking in some white neighborhoods. You really have to understand the times. I spent the majority of my childhood hearing adults speak very negatively about people of European descent. Most complaints were justified.

I remember being in our neighborhood park Hanna Homestead (land donated by Samuel Hanna), around the ages of 7-9 and teenage boys would get done playing basketball and start talking and complaining about white people. They would drive their selves into a fit of rage and we would all go to the park entrance on Lewis Street and they would hurl bricks, and bottles at any white person that drove down our street. I, like most youngsters would learn to hate our oppressor in the street and I would go home and learn to love everyone, based on Martin Luther King's philosophies which my Mother embraced.

My Father had a kind of opposite philosophy then my Mother. I would go to his store and hear him and his friends complaining about the White man did this, the White man did that. A bunch of truthful but extremely negative complaints. Hopefully you can understand the atmosphere at this time in our community. So the school bussing thing puzzles me. They sent us 12-15 year olds that far away from our families and homes and everything we knew into a land of people that were very divided at best on how they felt about us being there. I was called nigger at least four times a day. We kind of huddled together.

Academically my grades plummeted to C's and even D's. I went from a potential valedictorian to a slightly below average student. Overnight?

It took me years to understand what happened. Fortunately for me my Mother would make me memorize things like the state capitals, religious phrases, historical facts and mathematical equations that have helped me at different times in my life.

In Middle school, guitar was taught and the same results as in the past when I was in a music class. Excellent grades. Fortunately I got no criticism, but all the teacher had us playing were Beatle songs. I appreciate and respect the Beatles and their influence on culture. But I wanted to play some music like, The Jacksons, The Bar Kays, Stevie Wonder, Kool & the Gang, B.T. Express, James Brown, Ohio Players, Isley Brothers, War, David Bowie, Elton John, Eddie Kendricks, Rufus, Curtis Mayfield, Wild Cherry, Hall and Oats, Brass Construction, KC and the Sunshine Band, Average White Band, Earth Wind and Fire or LTD.

However I was in a room full of people that would rather be playing Kiss, Black Sabbath, The Eagles, Kansas, Rush, Boston, R E O Speedwagon, Jimi Hendricks, Eric Clapton, The Doors, Peter Frampton, Cheap Trick, Edgar Winter, Steve Miller and even groups like 10CC, ABBA or Blondie. At that time I knew absolutely nothing about those recording artists. So needless to say my mind wondered away from creating and playing music until I heard Rapper's Delight a few years later but that is another story.

I have always been a never give up type of person. I don't quit, I usually just take breaks. I remembered being the most nonathletic person in Middle School and decided I was going to be a professional athlete since I was no longer smart. I tried football and was on the bench deep. I tried basketball and was cut. I was pretty chubby. I went out for track and got last in every sprinting race I was in, I ended up being a miler. Best thing for me. It gave me determination, stamina, mind control and taught me to focus on a goal.

I thought I was Forrest Gump the way I would run. My knees hurt now thinking about it. My freshman year in high school I actually got to play in a couple football games. I got a tackle for a loss of yards and that was my biggest moment in football. Yay Dave! I was growling too.

In High School I ran cross country my sophomore year and started losing weight. I got in reasonable shape and decided to try wrestling. I lost so much weight so fast I was getting my ass kicked. So I quit and went out for winter track. Hey track never let me down even if I had inferior athletic ability. I lifted weights, stretched and ran to get ready for meets. I gradually started being competitive. I decided it was time to go out for Football. I was ready. I figured I could sit the bench my junior year and start my senior year. I had increased my strength, speed, on field awareness and vertical jump. I was cut because the wrestling coach I quit on was the assistant and defensive football coach. Color me fucked. I was cut again.

So track was the only sport I participated in that year. My senior year being this person that can't take no for an answer....I went out for football again. I was in better shape. Worked twice as hard and same conclusion. I was out running and hitting at least half the players on the team but same result. Cut. Funny thing the starting tailback told me I was getting the ax a few days before the cuts were announced. Back in middle school or Jr. High as it was called back then. I was introduced to woodworking, metal works and drafting. I did very well in drafting. I couldn't letter worth a shit, but I could make some pretty pictures. I never imagined at that time that drafting would occupy such a large chunk of my adult life.

CHAPTER 22

MY PROFESSIONAL LIFE

When I was hired to my first engineering position, I was hired so far down on the financial hierarchy in the company that there were entry level administrators or secretaries earning higher salaries than I was, and I was an engineering designer. There are several reasons for this within and outside of my control. As I stated earlier I had very little college education in the field. I actually studied Architectural Drafting in college. I only got the job because I was a descendant of NON (Natives of the Niger River Valley) via Affirmative Action and I did actually have some college drafting courses.

I was hated because I was a descendant of NON. I was surrounded by racists of some level. There was always someone there attempting to intimidate me, sometimes very successfully. It was obvious they hated me because I could just look around the room at different times and like clockwork someone would be staring at me and giving me a very hateful and hauntingly evil look. No one would help me become a better designer unless they were told to and then it would be with great reluctance.

Imagine a group of people letting you know on a daily basis they didn't want you there and you didn't deserve the job. I was only making $6 per hour so you would think since I was almost working free of charge, I could get some slack. I was isolated and hated no matter what I did. I had a supervisor who was stressing me out telling me not to tell his boss he was picking on me. My co-workers hated me because in my opinion

138

some young and bright white person deserved the job more than I did and that person went to school, graduated and had some sort of degree in their collective opinions.

They were being logical, I have to admit. I hadn't earned my place there. I was handed it for being a descendant of slaves. I felt all the animosity I could stand on a daily basis. People would complain about me for something to do or just too waste time. I was an ongoing constant source of humor and hate for them. This caused me to develop a very low professional self-esteem.

People would advise me to go back to school. Go back to school? I barely went to class when I didn't have a job and had time to study. I thought to myself that I hated engineering and the people hated me so I should start to be focused on being a business owner. My Mother had worked for the exact same company I worked for, for over 30 years in their factory and got little more than a few parting gifts at retirement.

I used to go to her building to have lunch with her. The days I would have lunch with her I would dress nicely so she would feel a boost of confidence around her co-workers that her son was in engineering and all the overtime she worked had paid off. It did in the long run, so I appreciate my Mother more than anyone can imagine. If it wasn't for the year she gave me in college this book would not be possible. About this time I made myself a promise I would not give my whole life to a company that could do someone like they did my Mother and were going to do to me if I decided to give them my whole life.

So many people work for the same company their entire life and die or become incapacitated mentally or physically within a couple years after retiring and the only time they had control of their lives there was some parental figure telling them to give up control of their life and get a job. I am guilty of being on both sides of this fence. So since school was out of the question and I lacked the wisdom to get a pay raise. I was stuck to paddle water indefinitely.

I had no clue what to do to achieve a pay increase.

I know now one must learn their job and show constant progress to achieve advancement and higher salaries. But I had stopped caring.

I lacked the work ethic to get a pay raise.

My professional morality was so beaten up that I couldn't care less about the job other than the paycheck I needed because I was in debt, with a mortgage, car payment, household items financed and credit cards. My heart was in my basement in my recording studio but it had turned into little more than an expensive hobby.

I lacked the confidence to get a pay raise.

I knew I was missing things needed to achieve a pay raise and that caused me to search for ways outside of the company to earn extra income. I sold radio advertising and DJ'd on weekends for the station and in night clubs. And I only felt peace when I was working in my recording studio in my free time.

While working at my first engineering job I saw Job Shoppers come and go but never knew anything about them or what they did. One was hired into our group, worked for a few months and left very quickly. I knew the boss liked him and heard him state how much of a loss he was. Just to give you an example of how much I was hated, the Job shopper worked about 60 hours per week the entire time he was there. Let's say his billing rate was $70 per hour. 60 hours times $70 = $4200 per week was what the client company was paying for him. I once worked 60 hours which equals 70 hours because I got time and a half for overtime: 70 hours times $6.35 = $444.50.

My boss went off on me for over a week for that and I finished the job. I never supported that engineer again and shortly thereafter I was put into a group with a devout racist for a supervisor. Lucky me. Both these supervisors worked for the same manager. I had a bit of a history with our manager. When I was originally hired by this company I was what they called a specification writer in actuality I wrote engineering change notices not engineering specs.

You need to know about several areas of a company to write those documents and I didn't know how to write a change notice let alone know what other departments were doing. Anyway this manager would always speak to me. I would always speak to him. On one of these occasions he asked me how I liked my job. I said very positively I liked it because at the time I did. He said good and paused like he wanted me to say something else so I took that as a moment I could maybe get a leg up. I said I do like my job but I would like to try that CAD. Which means Computer Aided Design, because most of engineering and drafting back then was asses and elbows, all hand drawn drawings on a big drawing board.

I remember old school shoppers telling me horror stories about sweat shops and the boss would come in and see workers talking and hanging out and say all I want to see is asses and elbows or the door is gonna hit you in the ass, to threaten his people back to work. People fresh off a job drought would be petrified in that moment. My future manager thought for a moment and said I think I can help you with that. A few days later he had me come to his office. He asked me if I wanted to come work for him and he would have me trained on CAD. I said YES! Wanted to say hell yeah! He then said well in order for me to get you into my group, I need to replace you in my fellow managers group. They work for the same Director. I need you to go out and find your replacement. I was like bet, I can do that. He then said if we hire them you get a $250.00 bonus per applicant and if they have a BSME or a BSEE you get $500.00 per applicant.

In some movies this is when an actor will break the fourth wall and say I got me a hustle and it's legal. I knew I had high school friends I could reach out to that had drafting in high school or had some college courses. I reached out to them and got 3 good candidates. I was excited. My wife was excited. It's on. One by one I spoke to all of them and they said they all were declined. I was like damn, what went wrong? The next day the manager called me into his office and said I thought you would have done this naturally without me having to actually say it.

His attitude was you act black. He briefly explained affirmative action's laws and how they affect government contracts in a defense contractor. He told me I need you to find some black people. My immediate thought was damn, really? Picture this. I grew up in a black neighborhood. Knew everyone in a mile radius of my house and their brothers, sisters, aunts, uncles and friends from across town. I mean the black part of town was like its own small town. Everyone knew everyone. It was a time when a neighbor would whoop your child for them acting up and call you, tell you what they did and you had a belt waiting for that child when they came home.

But this man just asked me to find a black person with an engineering back ground or some drafting type experience. This would be another fourth wall break and I just turn around and scream. This white man's crazy. Only a handful of black kids at that time went to college and it wasn't for engineering. I didn't even know what engineering was until I got the job I am attempting to recruit for. Well my wife and I went to the immediate pool and that was our families. First candidate was my brother in law. He had a math and computer background. He declined, but referred me to a common friend of ours who got the job and I was able to transfer into the CAD group.

That's when my engineering life really started and my innocence about professional racism caused my glass ceiling to come crashing down. I was shown job shopping three times before I got the bug. It seemed like an unbelievable pipe dream and I had so many negative doubts that I think W. Clement Stone or Og Mandino would have gotten frustrated trying to sell me on anything other than the status quo. I also didn't want to leave my wife, new baby boy and my recording studio.

But due to rising debts, lack of consistent business in the studio and me squandering all my income from Dee jaying, the third time was the charm. I had to get out of the hole I was in. So with approx. 4 years of engineering experience and barely any college study in the field, I accepted my first contract. I had no idea what I was getting myself into. All I saw were dollar signs. Looking back on it, that is very understandable.

Recently I was in one of my negative complaining moods and was telling my son how much I hated going to work with racists and the stress they caused me to endure. My son snapped and said write a book about what they have done to you. He also advised me that my life should be the back drop of this manuscript and after heavy thought I agreed to change the way I was writing this book. This change will make this book unique and in a category by itself. Often I feel like Thomas Edison, meaning; I don't care how many times I have failed in life I know I have to and will make something work sometime and I will not quit until something does.

CHAPTER 23

POSITIVE REINFORCEMENT

As a child I was taught by my family that we as black people needed to do twice as much to get half the credit. Having felt this, my whole life, this has become a habit and a sort of permanent way of thinking for me. I realize that performing twice as much to get half the credit is a science and this so called science needs to be practiced and perfected.

One needs to be aware of their work environment and know when to do more and when not too. Being patient and alert at all times will make one ready for those windows of opportunity that can help speed up your journey to a successful future.

It is a professional necessity to keep your finger on the pulse of your team or company's needs at all times. Constantly try to perform all labor and work efforts in the mind state mentioned just a moment ago. Constantly and continually in a habitual manner, update your mental studies and evaluations of your co-worker's and supervisor's personalities and moods. Developing a positive mind is a key ingredient that a great deal of rich and successful people has embodied to maintain a level of confidence to deal with the sine waves of life and industry.

Once a solid positive attitude is obtained the most important thing you can do for yourself is to maintain and improve your positive mind. This is your weapon for an attack and your shield for your defense. One must use their positive mind to succeed in their goals and endeavors, while protecting it from invading negative forces, moods and emotions.

The closest distance between two points is a straight line. Where you are now is one point, which you can call the origin point on the line and your goal or dream is the other point or your destination point on that line. See yourself at your destination points and in possession of your goals and dreams every day in your imagination. Practice this task on a daily basis. It can never be over-done, so do it as much as you can positively. Once your dreams and goals are firmly planted in your mind, imagination and subconscious mind, you will start moving in the direction of these goals and dreams.

Avoid negative moods, negative personalities and negative people so that your judgment is never clouded and you stay on the path, to obtain goals and be a success in the chosen field. Again, avoid the people that wish to slow you down, hinder your progress or destroy your path right out from under you.

Try to help others that deserve help along the way. You reap what you sow, so the more good you do, the more good you will receive. Do unto others as you would want done to you. The more success you obtain the more you should do your best to help others in whatever manner you feel comfortable.

It doesn't have to be monetary. Wonderful deeds can be done that are absolutely free, but can stimulate positive vibes and feelings that have immeasurable value to the recipient. Sometimes it's the thought that counts. Sometimes a perfectly timed warm smile can do the trick.

So never under estimate a good deed and its positive potential. Recognize and attract positive people. This is your people pool to find candidates for your inner circle. While examining the people in the pool, seek out the one's that live with compassion, empathy and respect and are also seeking like minds and personalities. Some people that possess these very positive traits maybe the hero, savior or I can fix them types. Protect these wonderful souls from the negative influences, because they are saints and sometimes they give more of themselves than they should.

Compassion can work against you if you aren't careful. Seek out the one's that live by the Golden Rule and the Two Way Street Principal. Recruit these individuals into your inner circle and lead and teach by example so that they can learn to do the same. Do your absolute best to protect and respect your inner circle from those that would do them harm. Your inner circle is your cabinet and you are the President of your own destiny.

Protect and respect your dreams and goals, because if you don't, who will? One must strive to go to bed every night knowing they did no human being negatively. One must strive to always maintain compassion, empathy and respect for the ones you care about. Constantly monitor if they have compassion, empathy and respect for you. On the event they lose one or more of these positive emotions, you must evaluate them to see if they can remain a part of your inner circle or do you need to perform a biopsy.

Even your inner circle can be caught up in sheep mode. When people are caught up in sheep mode, talking doesn't always work in the fight to help them. So you must remember that actions speak louder than words. One must lead with their actions.

I have done a lot of thought on the concept of sheep mode. People that are controlled by this concept have tunnel vision. Some even know what they are doing will hurt them and they are helpless to change their circumstances. I was like this with blunt cigars. They actually print on the package the negative effects of cigar smoking. I would read it and then get a lighter and smoke the cigar. I was and they are subconsciously loyal to Yo Gubna, even when things aren't as good as they should be.

Just recently an extremely intelligent lady that means the world to me and I love a great deal, thought because I wanted her to check out some books on curing a couple ailments she has, that I wanted her to quit eating Fast Food. This sent off an internal mechanism in her. She seemed to get upset with me. Another girlfriend of mine made the statement out of nowhere, "I am not going to argue with you." Since I am something like a Vegan, anytime I say positive statements about the health benefits of a plant based diet, some people do get offended and think I am campaigning for them to become a Vegan as well.

When you are in sheep mode, (as I am aware of because when it came to food I loved burgers, fries and vanilla shakes) nothing is more important than the taste that you have grown accustomed to. Not even health can cause you to do what's best for you when you need a fast food fix... Fried chicken does taste a hell of a lot better than a salad. Or does it? I believe our taste buds are programmed to the appeal of certain processed foods. Advertisers study humans to determine how to get them more addicted to their processed product lines. The more of these processed foods we consume the more we crave them.

It is said that in some fast food there are similar agents that have the same effect on the brain as some illegal drugs. They cause enjoyment areas of the brain to be stimulated when some fast food is consumed. People have to make the choice for themselves to take better care of themselves. You can't make someone do as you want them to do. That is slavery. You can lead a horse to water but you can't make it drink.

If you care for someone, you must let them live their own life. You can't live it for them. Just care for them. That is all they want from you and all you can do for them. They often say life isn't fair, so I say if we all must think for ourselves and not let the brain washing, programming and television commercials change our lives negatively forever. We need to follow and live by the two way street principal while utilizing the golden rule. Via these vehicles we can eliminate the possibility of a perpetual life of negativity. Stay positive my friend.

ADDENDA

-

ADDENDUM 1

HISTORICAL EXPLANATIONS

I wrote these next chapters because some people have the cards stacked against them from birth or their new birth, as in the case of someone from the LGBT culture. They in my opinion, and me being a minority, need a little something extra sometimes to make an end meet it seems.

Hate is a very powerful emotion. Hate is destructive and can have devastating effects on any situation. Some people are born with haters. Haters driven to kill people, but most defiantly willing to hold them back economically over the course of history. The chauvinist and or sexist, the racist and all those homophobes are three of the worse people on the planet. Thank God they all aren't extremists.

Women, minorities and people with alternative sexual orientations have to deal with prejudice, racism, sexist opinions, lower wages, rape, physical abuse, murder, discrimination, police abuse, public opinion, family pressures, unconstitutional laws and negative mind sets. Some ignore and act as if these people that hate don't exist in a manner that is almost insulting. Making statements like, "You are paranoid or don't worry about them they don't mean nothing", after the person insulted you. Sometimes the hate for these people comes from yo Gubna, as in most illegal drug laws.

- Some blame the person they hate for something they know that the person is innocent of.
- Some just look angry and mean at the people they hate and scowl at them.

- Some want to do harm to the people they hate. Some are and were such cowards, they would wear hoods so no one could see their faces; so proud yet so ashamed.
- Some want to stifle the career of the person they hate.
- Some want to murder the person they hate and kill their loved ones.
- Some just feel superior to the person they hate and could never believe that the person they hate has any real intelligence.
- Some, believe it or not, still want to own the person they hate like cattle again.
- Some use their money and influence to negatively affect the lives of a mass number of people in the group they hate.

These people hate most of all to be illuminated as the one that hates. To be shown in an accurate light. As long as no one knows they can be as hateful as they want to be.

The facial expressions can always give a negative person away and it is a telltale sign of who has hate and anger in them. The body doesn't lie. Voices do. One expression I started looking for is the "Oh shit, he,(she, they) are black or some other minority, a woman or gay", look. For me obviously it's the "oh shit, he's black", look. An even worse moment is the straight mouth position after you smile at them.

You should never care or worry about what people think about you. You have more important things to think about, you must literally have a FTA about anyone that speaks or acts negatively towards you. An FTA is a Fuck Them Attitude.

We all must develop emotional scar tissue and try our best not to be sensitive and emotional, but very logical about our place in this world. A clear non-emotional mind is the only way to battle prejudice or discrimination. You must be disciplined enough to only allow this energy to exist in your thoughts and never surface for any person to witness. Do not let any person know what you are thinking unless it is in your best interest. However, you should always be aware of the way people perceive you. Pay attention to your body language and facial expressions as well as those things in others.

Suppose you have a secret that could possibly cost you some extreme embarrassment or even your employment. How would it feel to be worried, concerned and paranoid that someone may find out each day at work? Suppose they did find out. How would you feel if you discovered several high ranking officials despise people of a certain religion and that religion just happens to be yours.

Suppose you looked white but were actually black and you hear through the grape vine that your supervisor has a history of firing minorities because he doesn't feel they deserve that type of employment. What is the point I am making? Imagine having something or being something that can't be changed. Imagine that being held against you professionally. Everyone has something in their lives that they could be victimized about. If we all attempt to not be the professionally sadistic type and deal with others as we would like to be dealt with there would be more harmony in the work force.

Being a Job Shopper and a single parent I had to either constantly enroll or withdraw my son from different schools until I broke down and home schooled him. This turned out to be a benefit for both of us. We both got educations we could never get in over 90% of the schools and universities in this country. I remember during black history month, I would always bring up topics to teachers that would make them get that "deer in the headlights" look. They would almost exhibit fear that they took a pledge to never teach the history of Africa.

I would say things like, "This is good; why can't they learn this type of thing year round?". Almost all of the teachers I would make this statement to were either black or empathetic. When I set out to home school my son I decided to start with everything about African people that they would not teach in U.S. Schools. My son and I studied the history of Africa from Antiquity to Apartheid.

We studied about the different nations of people that are the ancestors of the slave in this country. We studied about the richest man ever in the history of this planet. Mansa Kankan Musa, ruler of Mali. This ruler had so much money his slaves walked with staffs made of pure gold. When he did his pilgrimage to pray in Mecca, he stopped in Egypt and spent so much money that the Egyptians money system crashed and they switched their money over to his.

His nation accumulated their wealth from the sale of books and scrolls containing knowledge, such as mathematics, architecture, engineering, religion, philosophy, art, music and so much more. Timbuktu, the nation's capital was the equivalent of Paris, Tokyo, New York. Hong Kong, London all rolled up into one city.

A picture of Mansa Musa circulated in Europe of this man holding a small golden bolder approximately 9 inches in diameter. The monarchy of Europe saw this picture and heard of this man's vast wealth and sent emissaries to literally beg for financial help due to the living conditions of Europe post-Dark Ages. After a while the people of Northern Africa grew tired of these people constantly asking them for things and started saying no to them. The monarchy of the European countries grew tired of getting a no answer and gave their people the permission to steal from the Africans. After many negative events due to this change in policy, the Monarchy made this statement. "Go and take the land as if no person is there".

I believe at this point it went deeper and they were told these people were animals. I understand the logic. If you see a dog with a hundred dollars in his mouth what would you do? If you see a man with a hundred dollar bill in his hand what do you do? A good person would take it from the dog and leave the man alone. Thus in my opinion this is the origin of racism.

This same system was applied in this country during Manifest Destiny and on both continents genocide is and was carried out in order to take the land and the wealth. People were taught that the Slave was a savage, an animal and didn't deserve human dignity. Now I understand, with any criminal after the crime is committed one must erase all evidence of the crime and that meant permanently keeping the victims voiceless and ignorant which they did a very good job on the Black people in this country. This is why True and complete history is not taught in our schools. The criminal would literally need to snitch on his self. When someone has stolen and killed as much as this, do you really expect them to snitch on themselves? If you do then expect that 40 acres and a mule if you are black and believe any of those treaties with natives meant anything whatsoever. One name… Andrew Jackson. He had the art of deception and lying locked down to a science and mastered it. Ask the Cherokee.

Some people are just evil and won't change and because of this, subcultures have to rise up and start a revolution at times to make sure that their rights are not ever violated or taken. The problem with any American cultural revolution is in the U S, the struggle should not have been dealt with on the street and or on TV for other people and the government but within us.

The front lines of any revolution are in our own minds. The goal should have been to eliminate the philosophies of the Willie Lynch letter and any other evil philosophy that shows or puts another human being in a negative light, forever.

Two examples are the extreme products of Willie Lynchism are Uncle Ruckus from the animated TV series "The Boondocks" and the character Stephen from the movie "Django Unchained". Two black characters that hate themselves so much, they take the hate and aggression out on other Black people.

Where ever there is a revolution, you have people using the negative emotions abusively that are in power. I have no issues with democracy. I have a problem with democracy infused with capitalism in a racist, homophobic and still very sexist society.

ADDENDUM 2

WOMEN'S PLIGHT

In most cultures, women were and are looked upon as second class citizens. I think it's pretty stupid to treat the mother of children in a negative manner. These ladies should be edified and taught from birth to believe in themselves. Even today, in the U.S., women are still not treated as well as they should be. If you compare the salaries of men to women you can see this disparaging fact. Women had to march, protest and demand respect for hundreds of years before the men in power in this country would recognize them.

In the Middle East it is widely publicized that Arab women have no rights, must dress a certain way and have a different set of laws that apply only to them. I am very proud of the facts that in the pre-colonialist Niger River Valley section of Africa women were treated with respect taught to be confident and for all practical purposes, ran our society.

Niger River Valley African men were basically their wives back bone. We would gather and hunt food, protect the family from danger and negativity and be the ultimate companion to them. We were allowed to have as many wives as we could make happy and keep happy. In our free time we would just hang out with siblings, relatives and friends and talk and drink milk. Once I learned this, I realized so much about our people and the way we act. I also understand why the African woman is so bitter. She should be, it is a scientific fact African people were the first people on the planet which means the African woman is the Mother of all peoples, and just look how she has been treated. She was raped on a daily basis by slave masters in this country and her children parceled out like puppy litter. She has all the reason in the world to be bitter. Who wouldn't be under the same circumstances? In some ways women in this country were treated as badly as an African. When they strived to achieve more than just being a house wife there was always some chauvinist saying they are so beautiful and how they could make a man so happy being his wife and raising his children and being a good mother when she had ambitions to be a doctor, lawyer, author or some other profession that the men in power felt only they could do and no one else possesses the intelligence and skills to do it.

Insecurity can bring down a country and cause a revolution. Women were ready to revolt and probably would have if they didn't care about the man so much they were protesting to. As a race of people the American women were patient, never backing down completely. They always played a hole card, whenever they needed to turn the heat up on their lover and inhibitor.

A second-class citizen is defined as a person who is hated against, despite being a citizen or legal resident of the country or state. Even today women are still not given an equal share of the American pie in this country. They earned about 77% of men salaries in 2012, according to the U.S. Census Bureau. At that time, women working full time were earning approx. $38,000. Men were earning about $50,000. There was an increase by about 1 million more men working between 2011 and 2012, compared to the number of full-time women working, which remained about the same. The salary gap is worse among non-white people: African-American women earn about 69% of African-American men's wages. Latino American women earn a mere 58% of Latino men's earnings. Yo Gubna, is writing laws to help level the playing field in this country and help women live a better quality of life. House minority leader and California Rep. Nancy Pelosi and Rep. Rosa Delauro (of Connecticut's 3rd congressional district) are championing the Paycheck Fairness Act, which would help reinforce the Equal Pay Act of 1963. This Equal Pay Act contains some legal loop holes that allowed employers to pay a woman less for the same job a man was doing. Republican lawmakers are working against this legislation, saying they feel it will hurt companies and have a negative effect on the economy.

Most Republicans voted against the Violence Against Women Act. One could make the argument that some Republicans are and were male chauvinists. As with the descendants of <u>NON</u>, in the United States, legislation helps but does not cure hatred, ignorance or arrogance. On Election Day in 1920, millions of American women got to vote for the first time. It took activists and reformers nearly 100 years to win that right; The 19th amendment of the U.S. constitution gave women this right. Congress passed this legislation on June 4, 1919, and ratified it on August 18, 1920. The 19th Amendment also gave women reproductive rights, a domestic violence voice, the right to a maternity leave, equal pay, sexual harassment protection, and sexual violence support. Many times in history women have been raped and nothing was done to help her physically and or emotionally. This still goes on today in some countries. In a good portion of these cases the woman was looked upon as a liar and there was no prosecution of the rapist. So this legislation was a major legal victory for women in this country.

In the 1850s, the women's movement gathered momentum, but lost it because of the Civil War taking precedence over almost everything at that time in history. After the war ended, the 14th Amendment was ratified in 1868. This amendment gave Constitutional protection to all male citizens and the 15th was ratified in 1870, guaranteeing black men the right to vote. This seemed to irk the women's movement. I can imagine what they might of thought. You give an animal his man hood before you give it to the mother of your children. This would be a good argument for women at the time. Elizabeth Cady Stanton and Susan B. Anthony, two leaders in the women's movement, refused to support the 15th Amendment and partnered with racist Southerners who wanted the white women's votes to be used to counteract votes cast by African-Americans.

In 1869, this group was named the National Woman Suffrage Association and began to push for a universal-suffrage amendment to be added to the Constitution. Around 1910 states slowly started giving women the right to vote. Idaho and Utah had given women voting rights around the turn of the century. In 1923, the National Women's Party introduced an amendment to the Constitution that prohibited discrimination based on the gender of a person. This amendment was never ratified. Some white men around this time in American history felt like they were God in human form and everyone else on the planet was inferior to them. We have had Presidents that were card carrying Ku Klux Klan members. They were Warren G. Harding, Woodrow Wilson, William McKinley, Calvin Coolidge, and Harry S. Truman. So anybody that wasn't a white male had it hard. I briefly dated a very attractive blonde Caucasian lady when I was on assignment in northern Texas.

I was actually shocked she dated me. She seemed like the type of white lady that may not date a black man. She asked me one evening at her home, before we set down to dinner, if I disliked any group of people. I said no, I don't dislike anyone. I judge every individual by their deeds and actions, however if I had to name one negative group, it would be white men. She looked angry and disappointed at me. I calibrated and said c'mon Honey if they were a good group of people you ladies wouldn't of had to have women's liberation, black people wouldn't of been enslaved, lynched and brain washed and Native Americans would number in the 100 million instead of nearly being exterminated. She broke up with me that night, I believe over this answer to her question.

In other countries of the world, women have a different amount of rights. In the Middle East women are still restricted in a lot of ways. In Jordan for example, women are allowed to travel freely without having to get permission from their male relatives. They can hold public office, pilot aircraft, and work as police officers and join the military. Egypt is considered the worst Middle Eastern country for women's rights. Sexual harassment as well as high rates of female genital mutilation are common with The Comoros islands being the worst case scenario. Iraq is considered second only to Egypt in violated female rights. Discriminatory laws and an increase in human trafficking contributed to this. There are villages surrounding Cairo where the bulk of economy is based on trafficking in women and forced marriages. A UN report in April said 99.3% of females in Egypt had been subjected to sexual harassment.

Saudi Arabia granted women the right to vote and run for political office in 2015. 30 women are appointed to the Shura Council. The Shura Council is a political body that cannot create legislation and seems to have a weak political voice. It seems to be sort of a token government body. The Saudi government passed a law penalizing husbands for domestic violence, including spousal neglect. The law does not abolish previous laws that grant male family members authority over their female relatives. In the United Arab Emirates or UAE is one of the most socially liberal countries of the region and authorities have been active in hiring women for important government positions. However they will still imprison a woman there for something that isn't a crime in this country. For example a 24-year-old Norwegian woman was sentenced to 16 months in prison for having sex out of marriage and for consuming alcohol after she accused a co-worker of raping her.

In Kuwait, women earned the right to vote in 2005. In 2009, four women won seats in parliament. Women can drive cars and travel on their own unlike some other Middle Eastern countries. They also don't have to cover their heads or faces. It has been said that Iraq is more dangerous for women than when Saddam Hussein was in power. In Iraq there is no legislation protecting women from domestic violence. The countries present constitution requires that a quarter of all parliament seats and government positions must be allocated to women. Due to the religious institutions, women in some areas of the country are forced to wear veils and an abaya which is a long, loose fitting black cloak that covers the entire body.

In Syria women hold positions and offices in parliament as Cabinet ministers and one of the country's vice presidents. In the northeastern part of the country, women are forced to cover their bodies, including hands and faces. In other areas, where there is less religious control, most women wear the Islamic veil. The World Economic Forum, ranked Saudi Arabia 10th from the worse in its 2013 report, ahead of Cote d'Ivoire, Yemen,

Mauritania, Syria, Chad, Pakistan, Mali, Morocco and Iran. In Yemen women may not leave their home without their husband's permission. Abuses against women are not only limited to Africa and the Middle East, even though incidents in those areas are highly publicized more frequently than other areas of the world due to Christianity's hypocritical hatred for Islam. Even to this day the women of the Vatican City aren't allowed to vote. In Arabia and Morocco a rape victim can be charged with crimes. Many don't protect the victims of rape. Some even take a negative step further by punishing women for leaving their home without a male companion. Their crime is being alone with a man that is not related to her. She can also face charges for becoming pregnant from a rape. In Morocco 16-year-old Amina Filali committed suicide after a judge made her marry the man she accused of raping her. Asia and Latin America have also placed limitations on women's lives.

In some areas of India, traffic laws don't apply to women. In these areas women are exempted from that mandate like motorcycle passengers must wear helmets. This causes thousands of deaths and injuries each year. Women's rights advocates have said that this is due to the devaluation and disrespect of women. In the country of Yemen a woman is legally only half of a witness. To quote a 2005 Freedom House report, a woman's testimony in court isn't taken seriously unless it's backed by a man's testimony... Women are also not allowed to testify in court cases involving adultery, theft, libel or sodomy. All over the world and throughout history women have been done dirty. Again women mean so much to men; it seems so disturbing that men could be so cold to such a wonderful creature.

I really love women a great deal and enjoy the edification of the women that deserve it. I think that countries that have laws in place and on the books that hurt women should be prosecuted as if they committed a war crime. To me it is a crime of war; because anytime you mess with the Mother of man you are destroying the most important human being on this planet. If you attack the women you attack all of mankind. A woman can create a miracle. That miracle is that a woman can reproduce life. Men can only help with that process. Without her, we as human beings would go extinct.

ADDENDUM 3

THE LGBT FACTOR

LGBT - Lesbian, Gay Men, Bi-sexual and Transgender. I realize there is strength in numbers, but these are four entirely unique, very diverse and totally different sub cultures. Society seems to have a need to put people that are unique in categories with labels. All four of these subcultures get put in the same hat. Negative people then tend to make up horrible, unflattering and insulting names and descriptions for these groups of people. It is almost like they are black. Yet people describe them as Gay. Most of them if allowed to live life in a manner pleasing to them, naturally would become very happy and positive people. In my opinion, most homophobic individuals have bi sexual or even homosexual tendencies and acting out in a violent manner against innocent people is how they cope with their emotional conflicts. These people feel the need to embrace the negative emotions whenever they see a form of bi, homo or Tran sexuality. The term hate crime was coined to describe the types of negativity these innocent people were forced to endure. As with any human being that has been subjugated to human rights abuses and issues, I am proud of the way these sub cultures of society have risen and are rising to an eventual level of equal respect amongst all people and even Christians, who if were actually as Christ like as some of them claim, would of been the first to embrace the down trodden.

A lesbian is a woman that is only intimate, romantic or sexual with another woman or women. In my opinion some naturally want to choose another woman for a mate and some have been damaged by an abusive male lover and the arms of a gentle woman is a pleasure after being possibly beaten in some cases of domestic abuse. This subculture has made remarkable strides and are becoming more and more accepted and common in today's society. Some of my best friends in life were lesbians and I enjoy hanging out with them. When we were in Fort Lauderdale, Florida, we resided at a Golf Resort in a high rise building. In the suite next door lived a mother and daughter. Both were lesbian. The Mother obviously chose to be lesbian, but I believe the daughter always preferred women, but one of my male artist would get her sexually excited. We became very close friends. I almost signed her to my label, but she was never able to complete a record. The daughter had a very attractive girlfriend that practically lived with them. The Mother loved to go to Karaoke. So once or twice a week we would go to different Karaoke bars in Broward County. At least half of the people that sing Karaoke can't sing, but the beautiful thing is, no one is hating. There is no negative emotions floating around about anyone's talent. They used to ask me to go up on stage, but I would always decline, being a record label owner. Let me explain, God gave me a lot of musical gifts, however, singing was not one of them.

The term gay is in most cases used as a blanket label for anyone in the LGBT community; however it is most commonly used to describe a man that is only intimate, romantic or sexual with another man or men. In my opinion some naturally want to choose another man for a mate. Some have been damaged by prescription drugs that cause erectile dysfunction, a small or micro penis in combination with a woman's ridicule about the size of their penis or sexual abuse as a child. Others start identifying as the opposite sex as early as 2 or 3 years old.

At times throughout my music career, I have worked with dance artists. Since dance, club and house are the mainstay music in gay clubs, some of HHN Records artists have performed in gay clubs along the East Coast and New England. Our artist and dancers were treated with the utmost respect and literally treated like major stars (which can be a wonderful thing for an artist if it doesn't go to their head). The clubs gave my label and the artist management team VIP treatment. Most importantly they always paid early or on time and I never once had to chase them down for payment for concerts. They were extremely professional people in comparison to Hip Hop or Dance Clubs. Unless you are a major artist main stream clubs treat artist like garbage until they get a local following. So I advise anyone looking to perform, be paid properly and treated with respect, don't be afraid to perform in a gay club.

Bi-sexual - A bisexual person is a person that can be romantic, intimate and or sexual with both male and female partners. My son and I always joke around, although I know we are both pretty serious about the fact that we both would prefer a bi sexual woman or a converted lesbian as a lover and mate for obvious reasons. This is the only LGBT sub culture that even homophobic Hip Hop loves, readily accepts and actually embraces.

In recent years due to video being produced and sold and the internet, bisexuality among high school and college aged females has exploded into today's social and cultural back drop. Heterosexual men have always appreciated the site of two girls kissing and this desire had been used as a vehicle to start an industry. "Girls gone Wild" with its late night commercials, had almost all men dying to see one of those video productions.

On the flip side of the coin, negative emotions are very hindering and controlling. Bi-sexual men have created a secret sub culture or society called on "the down low". Hiding their bi sexuality from friends and family due to a reluctance to deal with the homophobic and negative emotions of others. Imagine meeting the man or woman of your dreams and not being able to tell anyone you are in love with them for fear of sexual persecution. Bi sexual men lead normal lives in the day. Some are even married with children. They can be masculine or feminine. Some actually identify as a woman in a man on man relationship, however living life as a heterosexual man in their professional life or home. This can go right up to cross dressing in women's clothing, make up and wigs for the lover for sexual scenarios.

Transgender and or Transsexual-There are two types—

- MTF - meaning male to female, and
- FTM - meaning female to male

They are people that identify as the opposite sex of their birth gender, psychologically. Although a large percentage of Transsexuals are gay men or Lesbian, I have met heterosexual men that were cross dressers or transsexuals and were sexually involved with only women.

A transsexual is not a transvestite or a cross dresser. Cross dressing is a fashion preference not a sexual orientation. Due to the advances in plastic surgery, transsexuals are looking more and more natural once they start their transition. At times I have had to go to gay clubs to book or discuss a concert or pick up money for a performance. I have met FTM (female to male) and I could not tell at all they used to be women.

They are divided in two categories. Pre op and post op, being before and after the surgery. Some seem to be content with breast augmentation and plastic surgery. Others get the gender reassignment surgery. I remember as a child one of my best friends was homosexual. He only liked other boys in the neighborhood. After sixth grade the only place I could play a piano was at my gay friend's house. He was a very accomplished pianist as a child; a child prodigy. He taught me a great deal about the instrument.

In my opinion because he was a developing transsexual, no one wanted to help him succeed at playing piano. That was the early seventies and religious black people were very homophobic and black children were far worse. Being called gay was like some kind of negative tattoo. Once one person said it about you, it was almost like it was politically correct for anyone to accuse someone of being gay.

This is where guilty by association is relevant. Because we were friends and both played piano, it was automatically assumed that we both were gay. Our neighborhood society was so homophobic and hateful that I made the selfish choice of ending our friendship. We were never very close after that. I went to college and he went out to California.

Transsexual male to females have an extremely difficult existence. Most businesses won't hire a transsexual if it is obvious they used to be a male, legal or not. Most are forced because of lack of opportunity, to become prostitutes, internet entertainers and porn stars, just to have enough money for housing, food and clothing. I saw my friend only a couple times as an adult. She died rather young from contracting H.I.V. and AIDS.

She was a child prodigy, a wonder and an unusually gifted pianist. I often wonder if she had some of the support structures that are in place now to help her, how much different her life would have been. Maybe I could be in an audience of a few hundred other fans enjoying one of her piano performances today.

As I have said often, the negative emotions should be eliminated from our very being. We need to exhibit positivity for every person unless a person shows a negative or hostile stance against us. If this happens one must temporarily use the negative emotions to defend oneself. The Negative Emotions have wreaked havoc when used against these four sub cultures. Hate Crimes have had many casualties and many victims over the years. Innocent people have been beaten to death for something that isn't the business of their attacker. Nor does it do anything to negatively affect the attacker's life. The Homo phobic person is a lot like the racist. Both usually are such cowards they feel the courage to physically attack someone only when they are in groups. It's usually someone that they estimate as not being able to defend themselves very well; an easy Mark or prey.

Fortunately for our society, some very positive people from each of the sub cultures have survived the evil that has chased these people throughout history. Here are a few positive products of the LGBT community.

These last few years of my life I have had a tendency to watch a lot of documentaries and biographies. One such documentary was on a gentleman named ***Harvey Bernard Milk***, who was the first openly gay politician to be elected to public office in California. He won a seat on the San Francisco Board of Supervisors. He was from New York City, but moved to San Francisco in 1972. He settled in the Castro District. He tried three times to run for a political office but lost all three prior to being elected to a post of city supervisor in 1977. He championed gay rights legislation for the city of San Francisco. He was assassinated by Dan White, another city supervisor on November 27, 1978. Harvey Milk was an icon in San Francisco and a martyr in the gay community. Anne Kronenberg, his campaign manager, once said, "What set Harvey apart from you or me was that he was a visionary. He imagined a righteous world inside his head and then he set about to create it for real, for all of us. In 2009, Milk was awarded the Presidential Medal of Freedom.

Langston Hughes was an extremely gifted African American Writer. One reason I appreciate him is his poem *The Negro Speaks of Rivers*. The poem to me represents the travels of the pre colonialism, slavery and present day African Man. Since rivers were a common means of travel, the rivers seem to represent the highways of the time. The people of Timbuktu also known as the natives of Niger or <u>NON</u>, were peaceful travelers, traders, teachers, writers, scholars and Islamic. It is very possible that these are the people whose eyes he was seeing the world with when he wrote this masterpiece of literature.

Ellen DeGeneres became a huge star after a Johnny Carson endorsement in the early eighties. She has hosted many TV award shows, a TV sitcom and a talk show that is one of the most popular of all time and as a female, second only to Oprah. She has written three books, and owns a record company called Eleveneleven. Ellen has won many awards for her professional work and charitable efforts. What she is most famous with me is for doing the Crip Walk when she had Snoop Dog on her show as a celebrity guest.

James Byron Dean was a famous Hollywood actor that died tragically in an automobile accident in 1955. He was still in his early twenties, but made such an impact on society that he is still very famous today. I actually grew up near the town where James Dean grew up. He was born in Marion, Indiana about 40 miles south of Fort Wayne. James Dean is today, something like an urban legend in film history and culture. Three films define his legend. "Giant", "East of Eden", and the classic "Rebel without a Cause". He won an academy award after his death.

Marlon Brando, is best known in the circles I run in for being the Godfather, Don Corleone. He was well known for his movie roles, like

"The Wild", "A Streetcar Named Desire"," Reflections in a Golden Eye", "Viva Zapata!", "Julius Caesar", "On the Waterfront", "Last Tango in Paris" and "Apocalypse Now". Brando was also an activist and supporter of many human rights causes for African-American Civil Rights and Native American Movements.

Ma Rainey was born Gertrude Pridgett in, 1886 in Columbus, Georgia. She started performing around the ages of 12-14 years old. From 1914, she and her husband were billed as Rainey and Rainey, Assassinators of the Blues. Blues music increased in popularity and Ma Rainey became well known. Around this time, Rainey met Bessie Smith a young up and coming blues singer. It was rumored that Rainey kidnapped Smith, and made her join the Rabbit Foot Minstrels.

Rainey was signed by Paramount Records and started working with producer J. Mayo Williams. Under her recording contract with Paramount, she recorded songs "Bad Luck Blues", "Bo-Weevil Blues" and "Moonshine Blues". She recorded more than 100 records in about five years. She was called the Mother of the Blues.

In 1924 she recorded with Louie Armstrong. About this same time she a toured the South and Midwest singing for black and white audiences. She performed with bandleader and pianist Thomas Dorsey and his band called the Wildcats Jazz Band. Some of Rainey's lyrics contain open references to lesbianism or bisexuality. In a 1928 song she recorded, "Prove It on Me", in this classic she sings, "They said I do it, ain't nobody caught me. Sure got to prove it on me. Went out last night with a crowd of my friends. They must've been women, 'cause I don't like no men". "It's true I wear a collar and a tie... Talk to the gals just like any old man. The lyrics reportedly are about a night in 1925 when Rainey's house was raided by the police for hosting an orgy at her home with women in her show.

These great individuals have blessed our world with their presence and vast talents. We owe them so much for what they have and are still giving us. These are shining examples of why we as a people need to quit hating.

ADDENDUM 4

WHY AND HOW COME?

This chapter is completely off subject and has almost nothing to do with this book, but to be honest I have a bit of a twisted sense of humor. So with that said every parent or person that has younger siblings knows what it is like to get badgered with questions by a child. So here I am being a little childish and a little...........sarcastic...... Sorry....

Why is the Earth polluted? Why are there guns? Why was there an American slavery? Why were Japanese people put in Internment camps during World War II? Why were there Crusades? Why were the Jews Slaughtered in Nazi Germany? Why was AIDS invented? Why is the Church a hypocritical society? Why aren't most American Blacks, Muslim? What happened to the Tasmanian Peoples? What does the Gatling gun mean to the Zulu and Matabeli? Why did King Leopold put the people of the Congo through that? Why did I write the previous chapter? Why was my Great-great Grandfather mixed? Should Native Americans be patriots? If you were one, would you be? How can a man fight for his freedom and take another man's freedom at the same time? How can a group of people hate another group of people for no logical reason? What was the Tuskegee Experiment? What caused the fall of the Aztec and Mayan people? If the Native Americans would have successfully defended their lands would there be pollution in this hemisphere? If cancer, heart disease, AIDS and Herpes are curable, how come the medical industry doesn't teach us how to avoid it and cure people that do get it? How come the national U.S.D.A. HDL levels are 200 instead of 150? Why are cigarette's legal but any other harmful product is forced out of business or forced to change their formulas for public safety? Why is Barack Obama really hated as much as he is? Why did Ted Nugent call him a Mongrel? Why are Hiroshima and Nagasaki famous cities? What does small pox infected blankets mean? What were the trail of tears? What does Algiers and an electric fence have in common? Why did someone blast off the Sphinx's nose? How could the church finance a war on Islam but claim to be obedient to God? Where are the other books of the Bible and why are they missing? Why does the American educational system suck? What are the ingredients of chicken feed? Why is there such a thing as a nuclear weapon? Why was cocaine made illegal? What happen to the Swahili People that caused their downfall from an economic power? What does the phrase forty acres and a mule mean? What happened to the seeds? What happened to the fruit trees? If a car can run on water and electricity, why do we still produce the combustion air polluting engine? Was manifest destiny wrong? Why is every area of the world that was put through some sort of European colonialism in turmoil now? Why are places European employers went to, just ruins now? Why were these people mostly referred to as discoverers when someone was already there? Why have people with brown skin gone through hell for the last 8 to 900 years worldwide. Why are there weapons of mass destruction? How can some people claim to be Christ like but are okay with war and capital punishment? What do Opium and the Afghan war have in common? Why wasn't the nine eleven disaster investigated the same way as other flight disasters? Why were federal regulations pushed aside and ignored with nine eleven? How come there are no leaked videos of any I SIS beheadings? How could a man of God molest a little boy? Why was there an American Civil War? How come Timbuktu isn't an educational Mecca anymore? Why didn't we learn about Mansa Kankan Musa in school? What happened to Patrice Lumumba? Was Cecil Rhodes evil? Why did the Tea Party chant off with his head? How many countries benefitted from the fruits of the British Empire and how many didn't? How come some people can commit murder and not go to jail for it? How come some people can publicly poison you and make a profit while doing it? How come the town of Ferguson Missouri has a majority Black population, but has only a few Black police officers? How come there are no major fast food chains with only health food menus? Why was there white flight? Why have members of the L G B T community been treated so terribly? Why do cops kill innocent people at times? Why do they profile certain people?

Most of these questions could be answered with one statement. The negative emotions. Just think about it for a moment. Suppose we could alter every question's subject to be positive or at least neutral, how much better a place this world would this be? How do you suppose it would be if everyone involved had compassion, empathy and respect for each other? How much better would your life be if you had compassion, empathy and respect for your fellow human beings? Sometimes I know it can be difficult to be positive, so if you can't be positive at least try not to be negative.

THE INFAMOUS WILLIE LYNCH LETTER

This speech was said to have been delivered by Willie Lynch on the bank of the James River in the colony of Virginia in 1712. Lynch was a British slave owner in the West Indies. He was invited to the colony of Virginia in 1712 to teach his methods to slave owners there.

[Beginning of the Willie Lynch Letter]

Greetings,

Gentlemen. I greet you here on the bank of the James River in the year of our Lord one thousand seven hundred and twelve. First, I shall thank you, the gentlemen of the Colony of Virginia, for bringing me here. I am here to help you solve some of your problems with slaves. Your invitation reached me on my modest plantation in the West Indies, where I have experimented with some of the newest, and still the oldest, methods for control of slaves. Ancient Rome would envy us if my program is implemented. As our boat sailed south on the James River, named for our illustrious King, whose version of the Bible we cherish, I saw enough to know that your problem is not unique. While Rome used cords of wood as crosses for standing human bodies along its highways in great numbers, you are here using the tree and the rope on occasions. I caught the whiff of a dead slave hanging from a tree, a couple miles back. You are not only losing valuable stock by hangings, you are having uprisings, and slaves are running away, your crops are sometimes left in the fields too long for maximum profit, you suffer occasional fires, and your animals are killed. Gentlemen, you know what your problems are; I do not need to elaborate. I am not here to enumerate your problems; I am here to introduce you to a method of solving them. I

In my bag here, *I HAVE A FULL PROOF METHOD FOR CONTROLLING YOUR BLACK SLAVES*. I guarantee every one of you that, if installed correctly, *IT WILL CONTROL THE SLAVES FOR AT LEAST 300 HUNDREDS YEARS*. My method is simple. Any member of your family or your overseer can use it. *I HAVE OUTLINED A NUMBER OF DIFFERENCES AMONG THE SLAVES; AND I TAKE THESE DIFFERENCES AND MAKE THEM BIGGER. I USE FEAR, DISTRUST AND ENVY FOR CONTROL PURPOSES*. These methods have worked on my modest plantation in the West Indies and it will work throughout the South. Take this simple little list of differences and think about them. On top of my list is "AGE," but it's there only because it starts with an "a." The second is "*COLOR*" or shade. There is *INTELLIGENCE, SIZE, SEX, SIZES OF PLANTATIONS, STATUS* on plantations, *ATTITUDE* of owners, whether the slaves live in the valley, on a hill, East, West, North, South, have fine hair, course hair, or is tall or short. Now that you have a list of differences, I shall give you an outline of action, but before that, I shall assure you that *DISTRUST IS STRONGER THAN TRUST AND ENVY STRONGER THAN ADULATION, RESPECT OR ADMIRATION.*

The Black slaves after receiving this indoctrination shall carry on and will become self-refueling and self-generating for *HUNDREDS* of years, maybe *THOUSANDS*. Don't forget, you must pitch the *OLD* black male vs. the *YOUNG* black male, and the *YOUNG* black male against the *OLD* black male. You must use the *DARK* skin slaves vs. the *LIGHT* skin slaves, and the *LIGHT* skin slaves vs. the *DARK* skin slaves. You must use the *FEMALE* vs. the *MALE*, and the *MALE* vs. the *FEMALE*.

You must also have white servants and overseers [who] distrust all Blacks. But it is *NECESSARY THAT YOUR SLAVES TRUST AND DEPEND ON US. THEY MUST LOVE, RESPECT AND TRUST ONLY US.* Gentlemen, these kits are your keys to control. Use them. Have your wives and children use them, never miss an opportunity. *IF USED INTENSELY FOR ONE YEAR, THE SLAVES THEMSELVES WILL REMAIN PERPETUALLY DISTRUSTFUL.*

Thank you gentlemen."

References and Inspiring Influences

References

The art of war. (2006). Place of publication not identified: Filiquarian Pub.

A Brief History of the Trail of Tears. (n.d.). Retrieved February 26, 2015, from http://www.cherokee.org/AboutTheNation/History/TrailofTears/ABriefHistoryoftheTrailofTears.aspx

Bible Gateway passage: Mark 11:24 - New International Version. (n.d.). Retrieved February 27, 2015, from https://www.biblegateway.com/passage/?search=Mark 11:24

Daniel 1:12-17 - NRSA - Bible Study Tools. (n.d.). Retrieved March 19, 2015, from http://www.biblestudytools.com/nrsa/daniel/passage/?q=daniel 1:12-17

The Final Call. (n.d.). Retrieved February 26, 2015, from http://www.finalcall.com/artman/publish/Perspectives_1/Willie_Lynch_letter_The_Making_of_a_Slave.shtml

Frederick Douglass, "The Horrors of Slavery and England's Duty to Free the Bondsman: An Address Delivered in Taunton, England, on September 1, 1846." *Somerset County Gazette*, September 5, 1846. Blassingame, John (*et al*, eds.).*The Frederick Douglass Papers: Series One--Speeches, Debates, and Interviews*. New Haven: Yale University Press, 1979. Vol. I, p. 371.

Greene, R., & Elffers, J. (2000). The 48 laws of power. New York: Penguin Books.

Hill, N., & Lechter, S. (2011). Outwitting the devil: The secret to freedom and success. New York: Sterling.

Hill, N., & Pell, A. (2005). Think and grow rich: The landmark bestseller-
-now revised and updated for the 21st century. New York: Jeremy P. Tarcher/Penguin.

Houston, P. (2012). Spy the lie: Former CIA officers show you how to detect deception. New York: St. Martin's Press.

Hughes, Langston, and Earl B. Lewis. *The Negro Speaks of Rivers*. New York: Disney Jump at the Sun, 2009. Print.

Lowndes, L. (2001). Undercover sex signals. Baltimore, Md.: Agora Books.

"Musa Mansa." Encyclopedia of World Biography. 2004. Retrieved February 27, 2015 from Encyclopedia.com: http://www.encyclopedia.com/doc/1G2-3404704660.html

Pease, A., & Pease, B. (2006). The definitive book of body language (Bantam hardcover ed.). New York: Bantam Books.

INSPIRING INFLUENCES

François-Dominique Toussaint Louverture
Basil Davidson
Malcolm X
Napoleon Hill
Andrew Carnegie
La Ruth Wiley
Samuel Wiley, Sr.
Samuel Wiley, II
Marcus Garvey
Martin Luther King, Jr.
Mahatma Ghandi
Nat Turner
Crispus Attucks
Garret Morgan
Howard Lattimore
Kwame Nkrumah
Patrice Lumumba
Haile Selassie I
Alex Haley
Berry Gordy

NOTES